BI 3668753 7

KV-171-854

The Pu...

Dan McCabe

BIRMINGHAM CITY
UNIVERSITY
DISCARDED

BIRMINGHAM CITY
LIBRARY
UNIVERSITY

methuen | drama

LONDON • NEW YORK • OXFORD • NEW DELHI • SYDNEY

METHUEN DRAMA
Bloomsbury Publishing Plc
50 Bedford Square, London, WC1B 3DP, UK
1385 Broadway, New York, NY 10018, USA
29 Earlsfort Terrace, Dublin 2, Ireland

BLOOMSBURY, METHUEN DRAMA and the Methuen
Drama logo are trademarks of Bloomsbury Publishing Plc

First published in Great Britain 2024

Copyright © Dan McCabe, 2024

Dan McCabe has asserted his right under the Copyright, Designs
and Patents Act, 1988, to be identified as author of this work.

Cover design: Muse Creative Communications
Cover image © Michael Wharley

All rights reserved. No part of this publication may be reproduced or transmitted
in any form or by any means, electronic or mechanical, including photocopying,
recording, or any information storage or retrieval system, without prior
permission in writing from the publishers.

Bloomsbury Publishing Plc does not have any control over, or responsibility for,
any third-party websites referred to or in this book. All internet addresses given
in this book were correct at the time of going to press. The author and publisher
regret any inconvenience caused if addresses have changed or sites have
ceased to exist, but can accept no responsibility for any such changes.

No rights in incidental music or songs contained in the work are hereby granted
and performance rights for any performance/presentation whatsoever
must be obtained from the respective copyright owners.

All rights whatsoever in this play are strictly reserved and application for performance
etc. should be made before rehearsals to Permissions Department, Bloomsbury
Publishing Plc, 50 Bedford Square, London, WC1B 3DP, UK. No performance may
be given unless a licence has been obtained. No rights in incidental music or songs
contained in the Work are hereby granted and performance rights for any performance/
presentation whatsoever must be obtained from the respective copyright owners.

A catalogue record for this book is available from the British Library.

A catalog record for this book is available from the Library of Congress.

ISBN: PB: 978-1-3505-3388-2
         ePDF: 978-1-3505-3390-5
         eBook: 978-1-3505-3389-9

Series: Modern Plays

Typeset by Westchester Publishing Services
Printed and bound in Great Britain

To find out more about our authors and books visit
www.bloomsbury.com and sign up for our newsletters.

Kiln Theatre presents

The Purists

by **Dan McCabe**

Directed by Amit Sharma

Cast

Gerry Brinsler	**Jasper Britton**
Val Kano	**Tiffany Gray**
Nancy Reinstein	**Emma Kingston**
Mr. Bugz	**Richard Pepple**
Lamont Born Cipher	**Sule Rimi**

Creative Team

Playwright	**Dan McCabe**
Director	**Amit Sharma**
Set Designer	**Tom Piper**
Lighting Designer	**Oliver Fenwick**
Sound Designer	**Tony Gayle**
Costume Designer	**Ruth Badila**
Casting Director	**Isabella Odoffin**
Voice and Dialect Coach	**Hazel Holder**
Intimacy Director	**Robbie Taylor Hunt**
Kiln-Mackintosh Resident Assistant Director	**Imy Wyatt Corner**
Costume Supervisor	**Emma Cains**

Production Team

Production Manager	**Alysha Laviniere**
Deputy Production Manager	**Charlotte Ranson**
Company Stage Manager	**Constance Oak**
Deputy Stage Manager	**Robyn-Amber Manners**
Assistant Stage Manager (Book Cover)	**Daze Corder**

Sound No. 1	**Andy Hinton**
Sound No. 2	**Jasmine Fuller**
Technician	**Anna LeClair**
Tech Swing	**Ella Purvis**
Wardrobe Manager	**Lisa Brindley**
Production Electrician	**Paul Salmon**
Lighting Programmer	**Tamykha Patterson**
Production Sound Engineer	**Jamie Taylor**
Production Carpenter	**Calum Walker**
Rigger	**Jess Wilson**
Draftsperson	**James Lye**

Set built by Footprint Scenery, SteelDeck Rentals, Kiln Theatre Workshop

Kiln Theatre are grateful for the support of the following for this production:
Autograph
Bobby Laviniere
Paul Anderson at Sparks

Cast

Jasper Britton
Gerry Brinsler

Theatre credits include: *Murder in the Cathedral* (Southwark Cathedral); *Jerusalem* (Watermill Theatre); *Scrooge*, *What the Butler Saw* (Leicester Curve); *Antony and Cleopatra*, *A Jovial Crew*, *Beggar's Opera*, *Tamburlaine*, *Taming of the Shrew/Tamer Tam'd*, *Richard II*, *The Jew of Malta*, *Henry IV Parts 1 and 2* (RSC/The Barbican/Brooklyn Academy of Music, New York); *Race*, *Private Lives* (Hampstead Theatre); *The Picture of Dorian Gray* (Abbey Theatre); *Who's Afraid of Virginia Woolf?* (Sheffield Theatres); *The Visit* (Complicité); *The Wind in the Willows*, *Troilus and Cressida*, *Summerfolk*, *Fram*, *Honk!*, *Oedipus* (National Theatre); *Rhinoceros* (Royal Court); *Japes*, *Becket*, *The Libertine* (Theatre Royal Haymarket); *Macbeth*, *The Tempest* (Shakespeare's Globe); *The Last Cigarette* (Chichester Festival/Trafalgar Studios); *The Father* (Chichester Festival Theatre); *Bedroom Farce* (Aldwych Theatre); *Little Shop of Horrors*, *Pack of Lies* and *Habeas Corpus* (Menier Chocolate Factory).

Television credits include: *Hijack*, *My Dad's the Prime Minister*, *The Royal*, *Heartbeat*, *The Cry*, *Big Kids* and *Highlander*.

Film credits include: *The Critic*, *Aubergenfeld*, *Rise of the Footsoldier 2*, *Blood*, *Anonymous*, *Morris: A Life with Bells On* and *The New World*.

Tiffany Gray
Val Kano

Theatre credits include: *Between Riverside and Crazy* (Hampstead Theatre).

Film and television credits include: *Silo, Generation Z* and *The Amateur*.

Emma Kingston
Nancy Reinstein

Theatre credits include: *The Band's Visit* (Donmar Warehouse); *Carousel* (Kilworth House); *Heathers the Musical* (The Other Palace); *Evita* (International Tour); *Children of Eden* (Cadogen Hall); *The Last 5 Years* (Minack Theatre); *Fiddler on the Roof* (Chichester Festival Theatre); *In the Heights* (King's Cross Theatre/Southwark Playhouse); *Les Misérables* (Queen's Theatre); *Priscilla Queen of the Desert* and *Grease* (UK tours).

Film and television credits include: *Sound of Musicals with Neil Brand*, *BKLYN The Musical* and *Been So Long*.

Richard Pepple
Mr. Bugz

Theatre credits include: *The Convert* (Gate Theatre); *They Drink It in The Congo* (Almeida Theatre); and *High Life* (Hampstead Theatre).

Television credits include: *Cobra*, *The Rig*, *The Family Pile*, *Bridgerton*, *Gangs of London*, *Line of Duty*, *Cursed*, *Motherland*, *The Long Song*, *Code 404*, *Krypton* and *Clean Break*.

Film credits include: *Beasts of No Nation* and *Radioactive*.

Sule Rimi
Lamont Born Cipher

Theatre credits include: *Blues for an Alabama Sky*, *Three Sisters*, *The Suicide* (National Theatre); *Force Majeure*, *Measure for Measure*, *Sweat* (Donmar Warehouse); *Jitney* (Leeds Playhouse/Old Vic); *All My Sons*, *The American Clock* (The Old Vic); *The Living Newspaper*, *Glass! Kill! Bluebeard! Imp!* (Royal Court Theatre); *Love and Information*, *Desire Under the Elms* (Sheffield Theatres); *Barber Shop Chronicles* (National Theatre/Australia/New Zealand); *Mary Stuart*, *They Drink it in the Congo* (Almeida Theatre); *The Rolling Stone* (Royal Exchange Theatre/WYP/Orange Tree Theatre); *The Odyssey: Missing Presumed Dead* (ETT/Liverpool Everyman); *Bordergame* (National Theatre of Wales); *Muscle* and *Serious Money* (Chapter Cardiff).

Television credits include: *Grace*, *Foundation*, *The One That Got Away*, *The Day of The Jackal*, *Classified*, *The English*, *Andor*, *Manhunt: The Nightstalker*, *Black Earth Rising*, *Death in Paradise*, *Birds of a Feather Christmas Special*, *Strikeback*, *Unforgotten* and *Stella*.

Film credits include: *Ear For Eye*, *Ashens and the Quest for the Game Child*, *The Adventurer: Curse of the Midas Box*, *The Machine*, *Elfie Hopkins and the Gammons*, *Daddy's Girl*, *Starter for Ten* and *Francis*.

Creative Team

Dan McCabe
Playwright

Dan McCabe's play *The Purists* premiered at the Huntington Theater in Boston where it won the Elliot Norton Award for Best Production and the Elisabeth Osborn Award for Best Play. Other plays include *Blame the Parents*, *Reptilian* and *An Old Love Story*. He is co-writing the screenplay for the forthcoming James Baldwin biopic, with Billy Porter portraying the author and civil rights activist. He is a graduate of Juilliard's Lila Acheson Wallace American Playwrights Program.

Amit Sharma
Director

Amit Sharma is Artistic Director of Kiln Theatre where he directed *Pins and Needles* and the critically acclaimed sell-out run of *Retrograde*. Before joining the Kiln Theatre as Associate Director, he was previously Deputy Artistic Director of Birmingham Rep, Associate Artistic Director at the Royal Exchange, Manchester, and Associate Director at Graeae Theatre Company where his journey into theatre began. Sharma directed two productions at the National Theatre – *The Solid Life of Sugar Water* (Graeae Theatre Company/Theatre Royal Plymouth co-production) and *The Boy With Two Hearts* (also Wales Millennium Centre). He also co-directed *Prometheus Awakes*, one of the largest outdoor productions featuring Deaf and disabled artists as part of the London 2012 Cultural Olympiad (Graeae Theatre Company/Greenwich + Docklands International Festival/Stockton International Riverside Festival/La Fura Dels Baus), and *Aruna and the Raging Sun* in Chennai, India as part of UK/India Year of Culture 2017. He is an international award-winning director of theatre and television. Sharma is a BAFTA-nominated director for his two films which were part of the *Criptales* season on BBC and BBC America. He also co-directed the award-winning BBC and Netflix television drama *Then Barbara Met Alan* (Best Single Drama, 2023 Broadcast Awards). He began his training at Graeae Theatre Company with *Missing Piece 1*. His other theatre credits include *One Under* (Graeae Theatre Company/ Theatre Royal Plymouth), *Cosmic Scallies* (Graeae Theatre Company/

Royal Exchange Theatre) and *Iron Man* (Graeae Theatre Company/ international tour). His other television work includes *Hamish* and *Thunderbox.*

Tom Piper
Set Designer

For Kiln/Tricycle: *Girl on an Altar, White Teeth*, *The Wolf with Snakeskin Shoes*, *The House that will not Stand* and *Red Velvet*

Theatre credits include: *The Duchess (of Malfi)* (Trafalgar Theatre/ Lyceum Theatre, Edinburgh); *The Scent of Roses, Rhinoceros, Mrs Puntila, Hay Fever* (Lyceum Theatre, Edinburgh); *Macbeth (An Undoing)* (Lyceum Theatre Edinburgh/Rose Theatre/Theatre for a New Audience – Scottish Critics Awards for Best Design); *Jesus Trilogy* (Dublin Theatre Festival); *Never Let Me Go* (Rose Theatre/Bristol Old Vic/Malvern Theatres/Northampton Theatre/UK Tour); over 50 productions for the RSC, most recently *Faith, The Box of Delights, Hamnet, The Tempest* (RSC); *Medea* (National Theatre of Scotland/Edinburgh International Festival); *Cyrano de Bergerac* (National Theatre of Scotland); *Endgame, King Lear, Hamlet, The Libertine, Nora* (Citizens Theatre); *iHo, The Haystack* (Hampstead Theatre) and *Cherry Orchard* (Bristol Old Vic).

Opera credits include: *A Midsummer Night's Dream* (Scottish Opera); *Orfeo* (ROH/Roundhouse); *Rusalka, Eugene Onegin* and *Don Giovanni* (Garsington).

Other work includes: *Blood Swept Lands* and *Seas of Red* at the Tower of London for which he received an MBE for services to Theatre and First World War commemorations.

He has won an Olivier Award for Best Costume Design for *The Histories* (RSC) and Scottish Critics Award for Best Design for *Twelfth Night* (Dundee Rep).

Oliver Fenwick
Lighting Designer

For Kiln/Tricycle: *Pass Over, When The Crows Visit, White Teeth, Holy Sh!t, The Invisible Hand, The Colby Sisters*, *Red Velvet* (also Garrick Theatre/St Ann's, New York), *Handbagged* (also Vaudeville Theatre), *A Boy and his Soul*, *Bracken Moor*.

Theatre credits include: *Dear Octopus*, *The Father and the Assassin*, *Blues for an Alabama Sky, Kerry Jackson, Tartuffe – the Imposter*,

The Great Wave, Ugly Lies the Bone, The Motherf*cker with the Hat, The Holy Rosenbergs, Happy Now (National Theatre); *The School for Scandal, The Magician's Elephant, Love's Labour's Lost, Much Ado About Nothing, The Jew of Malta, Wendy and Peter Pan, The Winter's Tale, The Taming of the Shrew, Julius Caesar, The Drunks and The Grain Store* (RSC); *Girls & Boys* (Royal Court/Minetta Lane Theatre, New York); *Lela & Co, Routes, The Witness, Disconnect* (Royal Court); *Clyde's, Sweat, Trouble in Butetown, One Night in Miami, The Vote, Berenice* (Donmar Warehouse); *Ulster American* (Riverside Studios); *My City, Ruined* (Almeida); *After Miss Julie* (Young Vic); *The Merchant of Venice* (Shakespeare's Globe/International Tour); *Reykjavik, Genesis Inc., Mother Christmas, Gloria, Occupational. Hazards, Reasons to be Happy* (Hampstead Theatre); *Carmen* (WNO); *The Sun, The Moon, And The Stars, Noye's Fludde* (Theatre Royal Stratford); *To Kill a Mockingbird, Hobson's Choice, The Beggar's Opera* (Regent's Park Open Air Theatre); *Into the Woods, Sunday in the Park with George* (Châtelet Paris); *Di, Viv and Rose* (Vaudeville Theatre); *Bakersfield Mist* (Duchess Theatre); *The Madness of King George II, Kean* (Apollo Theatre) and *The Importance of Being Earnest* (Harold Pinter Theatre).

Tony Gayle
Sound Designer

For Kiln: *Two Strangers (Carry A Cake Across New York)* (also Criterion Theatre).

As sound designer, theatre credits include: *Becoming Nancy* (Birmingham Rep); *Play On!* (Talawa Theatre Company/UK Tour); *Shifters* (The Duke of York Theatre/Bush Theatre); *Next To Normal* (Wyndham's Theatre West End/Donmar Warehouse); *Fan Girls* (Lyric Hammersmith); *Gatsby* (American Repertory Theater); *The Lonely Londoners* (Jermyn Street Theatre); *High Times & Dirty Monsters* (Liverpool Playhouse); *My Neighbour Totoro* (RSC/Barbican Theatre – Olivier Award and WhatsOnStage Award for Best Sound Design); *Pygmalion, Sylvia* (Old Vic); *Beneatha's Place* (Young Vic); *School Girls; Or, The African Mean Girls* (Lyric Hammersmith); *Greatest Days* (UK Tour;) *Disney's AIDA* (Holland); *Newsies* (Troubadour/Wembley Park Theatre); *Kinky Boots* (New Wolsey Theatre); *Playboy of the West Indies* (Birmingham Rep); *Legally Blonde* (Regent's Park Theatre); *The 47th* (Old Vic); *Running With Lions* (Talawa/Lyric Hammersmith); *Spring Awakening* (Almeida Theatre); *The Wiz* (Hope Mill Theatre); *Get Up, Stand Up! The Bob Marley Musical* (Lyric Theatre); *A Place For We* (Talawa/Park Theatre); *Blue/Orange* (Theatre Royal Bath); *And Breathe…*(Almeida Theatre); *Gin Craze!* (Royal

& Derngate); *The Living Newspaper, Shoe Lady* (Royal Court); *Poet In da Corner* (Royal Court/UK Tour); *Beautiful – The Carole King Musical* (UK Tour); *Salad Days* (UK Tour); *American Idiot* (UK Tour); *Songs For Nobodies* (Wilton's Music Hall/Ambassador's Theatre); *Floyd Collins* (Wilton's Music Hall); *The Wild Party* (The Other Palace) and *Lazarus* (King's Cross).

Tony won the Black British Theatre Awards Light and Sound Recognition Award in 2019 and 2021. He is a Wise Children Trustee, Stage Sight Co-Director and Founder of The Audio Cartel.

Ruth Badila
Costume Designer

Ruth trained at the University of the Arts, Wimbledon, graduating in 2020. She then landed the role of associate assistant designer at the Kiln Theatre, working and learning from range of amazing creatives, mentored by Tom Piper, until 2022. She hopes to contribute and respond innovatively to the rapid change of the industry, whilst also thinking of ways theatre can become much more accessible and representative. She has recently finished a year-long role at the National Theatre as an assistant designer.

Isabella Odoffin CDG
Casting Director

Isabella is a casting director from North London.

Theatre includes: *Our Country's Good*, *Antigone: The Burial at Thebes* (Lyric Hammersmith); *For Black Boys Who Have Considered Suicide When the Hue Gets Too Heavy* (Garrick); *Beautiful Thing, After the End, Extinct, The Sun, the Moon and the Stars, Sucker Punch* (Theatre Royal Stratford East); *The Collaboration, Klippies, In A Word* (Young Vic); *All of Us, Master Harold & the Boys, Three Sisters, Small Island* (National Theatre); *Word-Play* (Royal Court); *Moreno* (Theatre503); *J'Ouvert* (The Harold Pinter Theatre) and *A Taste of Honey* (National Theatre Productions Tour).

Film credits include: *How to Have Sex*, *On Becoming a Guinea Fowl*, *September Says*, *Transamazonia*, *Leonora in the Morning Light*, *I Used to Be Famous*, *Girl*, *Boxing Day*, *ear for eye*, *Blue Story* and *The Drifters*.

Television credits include: *Supacell*, *Missing You*, *Anansi Boys*, *DI Ray: Season Two* and *The Last Bus*.

Hazel Holder
Voice and Dialect Coach

For Kiln/Tricycle: *Two Strangers (Carry a Cake Across New York)*, *Mlima's Tale*, *Retrograde*, *The Wife of Willesden*, *Pass Over*, *The Son*.

Theatre credits include: *Blues for an Alabama Sky*, *Rockets and Blue Lights*, *Death of England: Closing Time*, *Death of England: Delroy*, *Death of England*, *Small Island*, *Nine Night*, *Barber Shop Chronicles*, *Pericles*, *Angels in America* (National Theatre); *Best of Enemies*, *2:22* (Noël Coward Theatre); *Cock* (Ambassador's Theatre); *To Kill a Mockingbird* (Gielgud Theatre); *Get Up Stand Up!* (Lyric Theatre); *The Glass Menagerie* (Duke of York's); *Constellations* (Vaudeville Theatre); *Death of a Salesman* (Piccadilly Theatre); *Caroline, or Change* (Playhouse Theatre); *Uncle Vanya* (Harold Pinter Theatre); *Tina: The Tina Turner Musical* (Aldwych Theatre); *Dreamgirls* (Savoy); *The Goat, or Who is Sylvia?* (Theatre Royal Haymarket); *seven methods of killing kylie jenner*, *ear for eye*, *A Kind of People*, *Poet in Da Corner*, *Grimly Handsome*, *Pigs & Dogs*, *Cuttin' It*, *Father Comes Home from the Wars* (Royal Court Theatre); *Mandela*, *Best of Enemies*, *Changing Destiny*, *Fairview*, *Death of a Salesman*, *The Convert*, *The Mountaintop*, *The Emperor*, *Cuttin' It* (Young Vic); *Clyde's*, *The Doll's House Part II*, *Marys Seacole*, *Love and Other Acts of Violence* (Donmar Warehouse); *Jitney* (The Old Vic); *Richard II* (Sam Wanamaker Playhouse); *Guys and Dolls*, *Girls* (Talawa Theatre Company at Soho Theatre/Royal Exchange Theatre); *Caroline, or Change* (Chichester Festival Theatre/Hampstead Theatre) and *A Midsummer Night's Dream* (Shakespeare North).

Television, film and audio credits include: *Drift*, *The Silent Twins*, *Aisha*, *Death on the Nile* (for Letitia Wright); *The Anansi Boys*, *Wool*, *Small Axe* (Steve McQueen anthology); *The Power*, *In the Long Run* (for Jimmy Akingbola) and *A Visible Man* by Edward Enninful (Audible UK).

Robbie Taylor Hunt
Intimacy Director

Robbie is an Intimacy Director and Coordinator and theatre-maker.

Credits as Intimacy Director for theatre include: *Strategic Love Play*, *Bury Me* (Paines Plough/UK Tour); *Animal* (Park Theatre/Hope Mill Theatre); *Fatal Attractions* (Tour) and *The Real Ones* (Bush Theatre).

As an Intimacy Coordinator, he has worked on productions for Netflix, HBO, Disney, Paramount, Amazon Prime Video, the BBC, Channel 4, ITV and Apple TV, with recent TV credits including *Big Boys*, *Mary & George*, *You* series 4 and *Mr Loverman*.

Film credits include: *Femme, Pearl* and *Red, White and Royal Blue*.

As a theatre-maker, he co-created *Pansexual Pregnant Piracy* and *Lesbian Space Crime* (both Soho Theatre) with his company, Airlock, and has directed *TUNA* (Tour), *how we love* (Theatre Peckham/Arcola Theatre/VAULT Festival) and *ERIS* (Bunker Theatre).

Imy Wyatt Corner
Kiln-Mackintosh Resident Assistant Director

For Kiln: *Pins and Needles*.

Imy Wyatt Corner is Resident Assistant Director at Kiln Theatre. She trained on the Drama Directing MA at Bristol Old Vic Theatre School.

Directing credits include: *The Last One* (Arcola Theatre); *Passing* (Park Theatre); *Scarlet Sunday* (Omnibus Theatre); *Duck* (Arcola Theatre); *BEASTS* (Edinburgh Fringe); *A Midsummer Night's Dream* (The Grove DIY Skatepark); *Humane* (Pleasance Theatre); *Walk Swiftly & with Purpose* (North Wall Arts Centre/Theatre503); *Baby, What Blessings* (Theatre503/Bunker Theatre) and *Happy Yet?* (Edinburgh Fringe/International Theatre, Frankfurt).

Associate/Assistant Director credits include: *Private Lives* (Ambassadors Theatre); *Relatively Speaking* (Theatre Royal Bath/UK Tour); *The Dance of Death* (Theatre Royal Bath/UK Tour); *Love All* (Jermyn Street Theatre) and *The Straw Chair* (Finborough Theatre).

She was a Creative Associate at Jermyn Street Theatre 2022/3 and an Associate Artist at Arcola Theatre 2023/4.

'Kiln Theatre has revitalised the cultural life of Brent and brings world-class theatre at an affordable price to people from all walks of life.' **Zadie Smith**

Kiln Theatre sits in the heart of Kilburn in Brent, a unique and culturally diverse area of London where over 140 languages are spoken. We are a welcoming and proudly local venue, with an internationally acclaimed programme of world and UK premieres. Our work presents the world through a variety of lenses, amplifying unheard/ignored voices into the mainstream, exploring and examining the threads of human connection that cross race, culture and identity.

'This place was a special cocoon. Now she has grown and blossomed into a beautiful butterfly.' **Sharon D Clarke**

We believe that theatre is for all and want everyone to feel welcome and entitled to call the Kiln their own. We are committed to nurturing the talent of young people and local communities, to provide a platform for their voices to be heard.

'I wanted to say thank you for creating the most diverse theatre I have been to. In terms of race, culture, class, age, everything – not only in the selection of shows and actors, but in the audience.' **Audience member**

Kiln Theatre, 269 Kilburn High Road,
London, NW6 7JR
KilnTheatre.com | info@KilnTheatre.com
🛆 ◎ X ▶ ♪ @KilnTheatre

Supported by
**ARTS COUNCIL
ENGLAND**

Registration No. 1396429.
Registered Charity No. 276892

Creative Engagement at Kiln Theatre

We create projects with and for people of all ages who live, learn or work in Brent and North West London. Local people are encouraged to have fun, be creative, discover a career or an interest in theatre, and have their voices heard.

Learning

We support students and teachers to access theatre through our Learning programme. We are passionate about making projects and productions affordable and accessible to local schools and we believe all young people should have access to arts and culture.

Arrive Build Create, formerly known as Minding the Gap, has been running at Kiln for 18 years. We work with EAL (English as an Additional Language) and ESOL (English for Speakers of Other Languages) departments in local schools and colleges to provide creative drama-based sessions for newly arrived young people. Young people are supported to improve their English, build their confidence and settle into life in Brent. The **Arrive Build Create Trainees** programme and **Young Company** offer opportunities for participants to develop their skills further. We also offer training and resources for teachers working with EAL/ESOL students.

Our Schools programme includes **Backstage Workshops**, **Continuous Professional Development** for teachers, **Teacher Previews**, **Resource Packs** and **School Residencies**. We also deliver **Fullworks**, a weeklong half term project which explores careers in theatre open to students from Brent schools to explore careers in theatre, and work **Placements**, in partnership with Further and Higher Education centres.

Participation

The Participation programme is for local residents who are interested in engaging in theatre as aspiring artists or audiences. We invite people to join in, socialise and share stories with neighbours. Developed through co-creation, our Participation programme listens to and advocates for the priorities, heritages and stories of local people.

Our Participation work is rooted in Brent & North West London and celebrates the unique cultural and artistic life of our local area. Activity includes: **12–15 and 16–18 Youth Theatre**, **Dementia Friendly Screenings**,

Kiln Masterclasses and **Winter Warmers**. This year, we launched *Celebrating Our Stories: the Kilburn High Road Project*, made possible with The National Lottery Heritage Fund with thanks to National Lottery Players. This three-year heritage-focused project celebrates and platforms the hidden stories of the High Road and the residents, artists, businesses and organisations who call Kilburn home.

For more information about our work and how to get involved, scan the QR code, visit **kilntheatre.com/creative-engagement**, email us on **getinvolved@kilntheatre.com** or WhatsApp us on **07375 532006**.

Support Our Work

Kiln Theatre is a proudly local theatre with a world-class reputation. We create bold and engaging work which amplifies unheard voices. We are committed to staging extraordinary theatre, inspiring the next generation of artists, and keeping our ticket prices as low as possible.

Every year, we must raise close to **£1 million** to keep our doors open and our lights on. Will you help us?

Become a Kiln Friend

From just **£5 per month**, you can enjoy:

- Access to priority booking
- Exclusive updates and insights from Kiln
- Invitations to special Supporters' events

You can also become a Kiln Friend at **Silver** or **Gold** level, which offers an even wider range of exciting opportunities.

Scan the QR code to become a Kiln Friend today, or visit KilnTheatre.com/Give.

Kiln Circle

The Kiln Circle is a philanthropic supporters' group that sits at the heart of our theatre. The Circle are given special opportunities to get close to the work on our stage and the artists involved in each of our productions. Donations start from £2,500 per year. If you wish to join the Kiln Circle or hear more about philanthropy at Kiln, please get in touch with Catherine Walker (catherinewalker@kilntheatre.com or 020 7625 0135).

Other Ways to Give

- Donating when you book tickets
- Naming a Seat
- Remembering us in your will
- Partnering with us through your company
- Introducing us to your Trust or Foundation

Scan the QR code, visit **Kilntheatre.com/give** or call our Fundraising Team on 020 7625 0132 to join our community of supporters today.

Registered with **FUNDRAISING REGULATOR**   Registered Charity No. 276892

Thank You

We depend on donations of all sizes to ensure we can fulfil our mission to champion unheard voices and to make theatre for everyone. We would not be able to continue our work without the support of the following:

STATUTORY FUNDERS

Arts Council England
Brent Council Warm Spaces
Camden Council Culture Service
The National Lottery Heritage Fund

COMPANIES

The Agency (London) Ltd
Bloomberg Philanthropies
Investec
Nick Hern Books

MAJOR DONORS AND KILN CIRCLE

Nick and Aleksandra Barnes
The Basden Family
Primrose and David Bell
Torrence Boone
Jules and Cheryl Burns
Mary and Jim Callaghan
Laure Zanchi Duvoisin
Dasha Epstein
Gary and Carol Fethke
Matthew Greenburgh and Helen Payne
Ros and Alan Haigh
Mary Clancy Hatch
Linda Keenan
Adam Kenwright
Jonathan Levy and Gabrielle Rifkind
Brian and Clare Linden
Frances Magee
Dame Susie Sainsbury

Jon and NoraLee Sedmak
Dr Miriam Stoppard
Jan and Michael Topham

SILVER AND GOLD FRIENDS

Sue Fletcher
Nazima Kadir and Karl Gorz
Frances Lynn
Alison McLean and Michael Farthing
Ann and Peter Sprinz
Rama Thapar

LEGACIES

In memory of
Harry Frank Rose
Gillian Hooper

TRUSTS AND FOUNDATIONS

29th May 1961 Charitable Trust
The Atkin Foundation
The Austin and Hope Pilkington Trust
Backstage Trust
Bertha Foundation
Boris Karloff Charitable Foundation
Chapman Charitable Trust
Christina Smith Foundation
City Bridge Foundation – London's biggest independent charity funder
Cockayne Grants for the Arts, a donor advised fund held at the London

Community Foundation
John S Cohen Foundation
The D'Oyly Carte Charitable Trust
Esmée Fairbairn Foundation
The Foyle Foundation
Garfield Weston Foundation
Garrick Charitable Trust
The Hobson Charity
Jack Petchey Foundation
John Lyon's Charity
John Thaw Foundation
The Mackintosh Foundation
Marie-Louise von Motesiczky Charitable Trust
The Noël Coward Foundation
Pears Foundation
Richard Radcliffe Trust
The Roddick Foundation
Royal Victoria Hall Foundation
Stanley Thomas Johnson Foundation
Theatre Artists Pilot Programme
Three Monkies Trust
Vanderbilt Family Foundation
The Vandervell Foundation

And all those who wish to remain anonymous.

For Kiln Theatre

Artistic Director
Amit Sharma

Executive Director
Iain Goosey

Associate Artistic Director
Tom Wright

Kiln-Mackintosh Resident Assistant Director
Imy Wyatt Corner

Producer
Lisa Cagnacci

Assistant to the Artistic and the Executive Director
Eoin McAndrew

Head of Audiences & Sales
Spyros Kois

Marketing Manager
Susannah Shepherd

Press Representative
Kate Morley PR

Marketing Consultant
Pam Kehoe, JMA

Box Office & Ticketing Manager
Mary Christensen

Deputy Box Office & Front of House Manager
Maria Koutsou

Box Office Supervisor
Josh Radcliffe

Box Office Assistants
Jonah Garrett-Bannister
Gee Mumford
Trevor White
Martha Wrench

Head of Creative Engagement
Romana Flello

Learning Producer
Imogen Fletcher

Participation Producer
Stella Taljaard

Finance Director
Michele Lonergan

Finance Manager
Daniela Baiocco

Finance Officer
Laisharna Anderson

Fundraising Director
Catherine Walker

Fundraising Manager
Stiene Thillmann

Fundraising Officer
Alannah Lewis

Head of Operations & Front of House
Simon Davis

Catering Manager
Angeliki Apostola

Catering Supervisor
Madison Leach

Front of House & Events Manager
Dana McMillan

Office & HR Coordinator
Annika Weber

Duty Managers
Moya Matthews
Laetitia Somé

Catering Assistants
Hannah Carnac
Zinnia Kerai
James Lloyd
Kerri Purcell

Front of House Assistants
Faizan Ahmed
Isabelle Ajani
Amaliyah Allison
Joe Barber
Roo Browning
Saoirse Byrne
Sara Elshohady
Martha George
Flo Granger
Berlyn Jensen-Wallace
Kirsty Liddell
Anna Lines
Willa Main
Temi Majekodunmi
Lois Pearson
Rawdat Quadri
Riley Reed
Jacqueline Reljic
Sandip Valgi
Romario Williams
Martha Wrench
Amina Zebiri

Security Officer
Nagah Elshohady

Cleaning Manager
Ragne Kaldoja

Cleaners
Selide Ahanmada
Theresa Desmond
Jose Luz
Joslette Williamson

IT Consultant
Richard Lucas

Head of Production
Alysha Laviniere

Head of Lighting & Sound
Paul Salmon

Company Manager
Katie Bachtler

Technical & Facilities Manager
Dave Judd

Production Coordinator
Muriel de Palma

Cinema Technician & Programme Administrator
Emmett Cruddas

Cinema Consultant
Duncan Carson

Board of Trustees
Pippa Adamson
Michael Berg
Sabine Chalmers (Chair)
Louis Charalambous
Heather Doughty
Natasha Gordon
Katie Haines
Alastair Levy

The Purists

Characters

Gerry Brinsler, *male, sixties, white*
Lamont Born Cipher, *male, late forties, black*
Mr. Bugz, *male, late forties, black*
Val Kano, *female, twenties, Puerto Rican*
Nancy Reinstein, *female, twenties, white*

Setting

The stoop of a building in Sunnyside, Queens. Also Gerry's apartment. June. Now.

Preshow

Two turntables and a microphone are preset on stage. A few minutes before curtain, **Mr. Bugz** *enters and talks to the audience. He can improvise lines like "What up, what up, ya'll ready to have a good time, put your hands in the air, wave 'em like you just don't care" and other old school hip-hop catch phrases; anything to get the audience hyped and making noise.*

Then he spins a couple tracks and does some scratches, showing the audience his skills on the 1s and 2s. Then he reads the "Turn off all cellphones" announcement and tells them to enjoy the show.

Then he exits.

Act One

We're in Sunnyside, Queens. Summer. Now.

The setting has two levels. The lower level is a single, residential street in Sunnyside. Center stage is the entrance to a five-story walk-up building. Most of our action will take place on the stoop of the building; the five or six steps that lead up to the front door. Maybe there are some makeshift chairs next to the stoop; an empty crate, a cement block, things like that.

Far stage right is the very end of some scaffolding, implying that construction is being done to another building off stage.

The second level is **Gerry Brinsler**'s *apartment. His apartment is on the second floor of the building. Next door is stage right of the second level there is a sole window, which represents* **Mr. Bugz**'s *apartment, although we never see anything inside.*

As the lights come up, **Gerry Brinsler**, *sixties, a man with a permanent scowl on his face, is meandering around his messy apartment.*

Gerry *looks hung over. Because he is. He is often hung over. He goes to his record player and puts on a record, tilts his head back, and takes a breath. The music comes on: it's "Getting to Know You" from the original* The King and I *soundtrack. He exhales another deep breath, as if the sound of this music alone is alleviating his massive headache. He loves this. It is the best part of his day.*

But then we hear another sound. Something faint in the distance. **Gerry** *begins to hear it too and is not pleased.*

The sound gradually gets louder. It is the sound of the Pete Rock remix to Public Enemy's "Shut 'Em Down," coming from the retro boombox of **Lamont Born Cipher**, *late forties, who has just entered from stage right under the scaffolding. The music is now on full blast and has completely drowned out* The King and I.

Gerry *looks out his window with an angry growl. Maybe he tries to shout something but it is of no use, the music is too loud.* **Lamont** *knows the music is too loud. So he turns it up even more.*

Gerry*, much to his chagrin, turns off the record player and angrily stomps his way off stage back into his bedroom just as* **Mr. Bugz***, late forties, exits out of the building to greet his friend* **Lamont***, who has just placed the boombox next to the stoop.*

They give each other a pound and start to chat inaudibly as the music continues to play.

Then there is a lightning-fast blackout with the lights immediately coming back on again and the music from the boombox shifting, indicating a quick leap forward in time.

It's about a half hour later. The music plays very low from the boombox. **Bugz** *and* **Lamont** *chill on the stoop, in mid-conversation.*

Lamont   Get the fuck outta here—

Mr. Bugz (*shrugging, as in "sorry"*)   King of hip-hop—

Lamont   How? Howwwww?

Mr. Bugz (*listing with his fingers*)   Lyrically—

Lamont   Pshhh.

Mr. Bugz   His respect for the craft. His *dedication* to the craft—

Lamont   So what?

Mr. Bugz   *And* he's the number one—who's sold more albums than Eminem?

Lamont   So what?

Mr. Bugz   *"So what?"*

Lamont   So. / What.

Mr. Bugz   A hundred *million* albums, worldwide.

Gerry *comes out of the building, takes out a cigarette, plops it into his mouth. Searches for a lighter in his pockets.*

Lamont   Oh, so whoever *sells* the most, that's the uh, uh, / uh—

Mr. Bugz   It's not *everything*—

Lamont   —that's the *parameter* for who's the best?

Mr. Bugz   No, but you still gotta / consider that—

Lamont   'Cause then Vanilla Ice would be number two or three or some shit.

Mr. Bugz   Is it *all* that matters, nah, but is it a factor, yeah, hell yeah.

Gerry *can't find his lighter.*

Gerry   Goddamnit.

He heads back inside.

Lamont   You outta your mind, man.

Mr. Bugz   Like I said—he has shown the craft a lot of respect, he pays homage—(*Reaches into his pocket just as* **Gerry** *is going back into the building.*)—yo, Gerry I got a lighter right—

The door has shut.

Mr. Bugz   That man is hung over.

Lamont   "Respect for the craft" who gives a fuck!

Bugz *laughs.*

Lamont   Jay-Z don't got respect for the craft? Biggie ain't had respect / for the—

Mr. Bugz   Biggie ain't give a fuck about no craft, dawg, he was about that paper, that's it.

Lamont   Aight, yeah, maybe that's true.

Mr. Bugz   We did a show in—I wanna say North Carolina—this was like mid-'94? He told me straight up, he said (*doing a Biggie impression*) "Yo, Bugz, I'm only doing this shit cause I'm nice and I can make more money than if I was hustling." I remember being on stage, putting on the record, listening to him rhyme his *ass* off, I'm like, "Goddamn he don't even *care* about this shit!"

Lamont   Well, respect for the craft or not Biggie is *better* / than Eminem—

Mr. Bugz   Oh, obviously / I ain't debating that-

Lamont   *Jay-Z* is better than Eminem, 2Pac, Nas, shit my *nephew* is better than Eminem. The young god Hassan Power, I been tellin' you about.

Small pause. **Bugz** *looks confused.*

Lamont   I sent you a couple of his tracks. Like two weeks ago.

Mr. Bugz (*remembering*)   *Damn, that's right.*

Lamont   You ain't listen to that shit?

Bugz *shakes his head no.*

Lamont   Why not?

Mr. Bugz   I don't know, man, during my break from the radio station I haven't really been listening to *anything* new to be honest.

Lamont   Word? Well, when you *do* listen you'll see what I'm talking about.

Gerry *reenters, lights his cigarette.*

Lamont   Mattafact, he got a show this Monday . . .

Mr. Bugz   I'll try, man, you know me and commitments, aight, talk to my ex-wife.

Lamont *acknowledges* **Gerry**'s *presence for the first time.*

Lamont   What about you, Gerry with a G? You free this Monday, you wanna come listen to my nephew spit that raw shit?

Gerry   How about this? You come over my place, I'll make us margaritas and we listen to *Hello Dolly*?

Lamont *and* **Bugz** *crack up, give each other a pound.*

Lamont   Gerry with a *G*. My man!

Gerry   The one morning . . . the *one* morning . . . (*pointing to scaffolding*) . . . I don't wake up to the sound of that *fucking* jackhammer, you two just have to play your *god awful* music down here?

Lamont (*looking at his watch*)   This motherfucker says morning when it's 2 p.m.

Mr. Bugz   You hung over?

Gerry (*barking*)   Of course I am!

Bugz *and* **Lamont** *laugh.*

Mr. Bugz   What you do last night?

Gerry   What *didn't* I do?

They laugh again.

Lamont   I don't even wanna *know* what that means.

Mr. Bugz (*just remembering*)   Oh, yo, did you give one of them fuckin' kids my number?

Gerry   What kids?

Mr. Bugz   Them kids that *work* for you. Ever since that goddamn *musical* you took me to I been getting phone calls off the hook. They be like, "Is this Mr. Brandon Shaw?" I'm like, "Yeah." They're like, "This is so and so you saw . . . "—whatever the fuck that show was—"we want you to buy more." I'm like, "Yo, I don't wanna see no more goddamn *musicals*, I saw the one and that's it." Then I hang up. Then like two hours later they just call me again.

Gerry   That's impossible.

Mr. Bugz   You think I'm lying?

Gerry   You were my guest—how did they—

Mr. Bugz   That's what I'm asking you.

Lamont (*confused*)   Ya'll went to a musical together?

Gerry   When we were at the box office did you give them your credit card or—

Mr. Bugz   Hell no!

Gerry   And you didn't fill out any—

Mr. Bugz   No, no, no.

Lamont   Yo, ya'll went to a musical together?

Mr. Bugz   Yeah, he took me to see this—I was just kicking it out here and his friend bailed on him, he was like "You wanna come see this," I had nothing to do, I was like, "Fuck it, let's do this."

Lamont   How was it?

Mr. Bugz   It was pretty good.

Gerry   NO IT WASN'T, IT WAS TERRIBLE! JESUS CHRIST, ERGHHH!

Lamont and **Bugz** *laugh again, give each other a pound. They find* **Gerry** *very amusing.*

Lamont   Yo, don't you *work* for this theater?

Gerry   Yeah, so?

Lamont (*to* **Bugz**)   He keeps it real.

Mr. Bugz (*agreeing*)   Man keeps it real.

Gerry   *Ugggh.* That show made me wanna *murder* somebody. And by *somebody* I mean the people that wrote it.

Lamont   What was so bad about it?

Gerry *takes a moment, struggling to find the words.*

Gerry   *Everything*.

Mr. Bugz   That main chick had a good voice, don't even front about that, Gerry.

Gerry   She had a *decent* voice. Okay? It was *decent*. Jesus, people act as if she's the new messiah of musical theater. I'm sorry, but Judy Garland she is *not*.

Lamont   Yo, Gerry, who you think's the king of hip-hop?

Gerry   Oh, go fuck yourself.

Lamont *and* **Bugz** *laugh again, give each other another pound.*

Gerry *checks something on his phone.*

Mr. Bugz   You just a hater, Gerry.

Lamont   Don't ever be asking *me* to go to no musical with you, bruh.

Gerry (*as he scrolls on his phone*)   Don't worry, you're not exactly top of my list.

Lamont   I don't even wanna be *on* the list.

Gerry   You're not even on the *wait* list.

Lamont   Okay good.

Gerry (*re: iPhone*)   Uhp, good news, boys! The Queen's horse has qualified for the Epsom Oaks. (*Looking up to the heavens.*) So, I'm sure she'd be very happy about that.

Lamont   Can I ask you a real question? What exactly did Queen Elizabeth do?

Gerry (*shocked and insulted*)   What did she *do*? She *ruled*! What do *you* do?

Lamont *and* **Bugz** *laugh, give each other a pound.*

Gerry   I'd like you two boys to remember that the Queen was ninety-six years old when she died. Ninety-six! And until her final breath, she got out of bed every day and she did her job.

Lamont   Oh, that's interesting, Gerry, you've never reminded / us of that before.

Gerry   A magnificent reign! An absolutely mag*nifi*cent reign! From the age of twenty-five to the age of ninety fucking six! And did she ever complain? Not once. Did she ever sleep in? *Not once*. She got up and she went to work *every day*. No excuses.

Lamont   Yeah, the Queen was a gangsta, we get that.

Gerry   So, I don't wanna hear any more whining from you two, okay?

Lamont (*to* **Bugz**)   Speaking a old ladies, how's your mom doing, man?

Mr. Bugz   Pshh. You ever see that movie um . . . (*Snapping his fingers, trying to remember.*) . . . with what's her name, my homegirl from *Boogie Nights*?

Gerry (*he hates that movie*)   Ugh.

Lamont   Who, Heather Graham?

Mr. Bugz   Nah, the girl—the porn star, the first chick Mark / Wahlberg fucks . . .

Lamont   Oh, um, Julianna Margulies.

Gerry   Moore!

Mr. Bugz   Moore, Julianne Moore, yeah. You see that movie with her where she loses her memory?

Lamont   Nah.

Mr. Bugz   Well, that's what it's like with my mom. Great movie, by the way, sad as hell though.

Gerry   Have you ever heard of a little film called *On Golden Pond*? Henry Fonda, Jane Fonda, Katharine Hepburn? *That's* a movie.

Lamont   Yo, you wanna know a sad fucking movie? *Requiem for a Dream*.

Mr. Bugz   Oh hell yeah.

Lamont   It was on HBO the other day, I'm like, "Yo, this shit is too much for me, man."

Mr. Bugz   That's a one-viewing movie for sure, you don't wanna watch that shit more than once.

Lamont   Yeah, I feel that.

Gerry   Oh! Speaking of . . . Bugz, you're not gonna believe this, but last night . . . I had an erotic dream about you.

Mr. Bugz	**Lamont**
Whoa, whoa, whoa.	Yo, come on, man . . .

Gerry   What?

Mr. Bugz	**Lamont**
How you gonna say	You take shit too far, Gerry.
that to another grown man?	

Gerry   Oh, gimme a god / damn break.

Lamont   You *know* we don't wanna hear / shit like that.

Mr. Bugz   You *know* that, keep your fuckin' thoughts to / yourself sometimes.

Gerry   It was a *dream*! It wasn't real, it's not like I actually wanna have—

Lamont	**Mr. Bugz**
Chill, chill, chill.	Don't even say that shit, bro,
	just don't say it.

Gerry   Oh, you two are *pathetic*.

Mr. Bugz   And you lucky, my man.

Lamont   *Very* lucky.

Gerry   Lucky how?

Mr. Bugz	**Lamont**
That you're talking to us and not some other goons that we know.	That we tolerate you—yeah exactly.

Mr. Bugz You just need to watch your mouth sometimes, that's all.

Lamont That's all!

Gerry Oh, well, excuuuuuuuuussse me. (*Doing condescending baby talk.*) Did I upset you? Did I make you uncomfortable?

Lamont Yo, you just gonna get your teeth knocked out one day.

Gerry Oh, I couldn't care less. You think I'm afraid? You think I'm afraid of anything?

Lamont (*shaking his head*) Yo—

Gerry I say whatever I want to whoever I want, okay? No one intimidates me. Yesterday on the subway there were these two goddamn *thugs* spinning their legs around, hanging on top of the thing, I said, "HEY! Get down from there, you're gonna kick someone in the goddamn head." Goddamn *animals*! I speak the truth. I keep it real.

Silence.

What?

Mr. Bugz You're a bigot, that's what.

Gerry Excuse me?

Mr. Bugz Come on, Mr. Keep It Real, keep it real with us, you don't respect black people.

Lamont Facts.

Gerry *What?*

Mr. Bugz Keep it real, Gerry.

Gerry I don't resp—

Lamont   You don't respect *hood* motherfuckas.

Mr. Bugz   That's absolutely right. Yeah, you like the Sidney Poitiers of the world, no doubt, but when it comes to motherfuckers from the hood? When it comes to, you know—

Lamont   Poor people.

Mr. Bugz   *Poor black people*, you have a genuine dislike in your heart for poor black people. Just admit it, yo, there are a lot of racist motherfuckers who feel like you feel, you ain't alone.

Pause.

Gerry   I am very . . . VERY . . . offended by what you're saying right now.

Mr. Bugz   My man. I don't like you calling a young black kid a thug. Okay? Or an *animal,* are you serious? You watch Fox News, Gerry?

Gerry   *Excuse me?*

Mr. Bugz   You be watching Fox News? 'Cause that's the kinda rhetoric they be using on that station. Thugs, animals . . .

Lamont   Code words—

Mr. Bugz   All code words, the same mothefuckin' code words you just used to describe a young black kid on the train.

Gerry   Who said he was black?

Pause.

Gerry   A-ha! A-HA! *Whoever* said that?

Another pause.

Mr. Bugz   Well, was he?

Gerry   Well, yes, he was, but *you* didn't know that.

Mr. Bugz   Just own your shit, Gerry, that's all I'm saying.

Lamont   Yeah, cause when you say thug we all know what you really sayin'.

Mr. Bugz   Straight up.

Pause.

Gerry   *I'm* a racist? Me? Do you know how many black men I've had sex with? / Thousands! Do you hear me? Thousands!

Mr. Bugz	**Lamont**
Seriously? Seriously?	How many times we gotta tell you this, man?

Val Kano *enters from under the scaffolding. She's riding on a two-wheel Segway.*

Val   I swear to God, I could hear ya'll arguing from 46th Avenue.

Gerry (*to* **Lamont**)   *You* gotta lotta nerve, you know that? With the amount of venom I've heard spewed out of your mouth, Mr. Kill Whitey.

Lamont (*laughing*)   Yo, you have never in your entire life heard me say the words "Kill Whitey."

Gerry   Well, I've heard / you say a lot of—

Lamont   *No one* says "Kill Whitey" anymore, man, this ain't 1972.

Val   Yo, Gerry with a G, we doing business or what?

Gerry *reaches into his pocket, but can't find his wallet.*

Gerry   Oh, Jesus, I left my goddamn wallet up—WHAT IS WRONG WITH THIS WORLD!

Val   Mattafact I gotta take a piss anyway so . . .

Lamont (*quietly and playfully*)   Wash yo hands . . .

Gerry   Oh, whatever, come on up.

Val *follows* **Gerry** *up the steps.*

Mr. Bugz   What, no love?

Val   Oh, my bad.

She goes to give **Mr. Bugz** *a hug but he goes in for a pound, so it's kind of awkward.*

Val   Oh, I thought—we not huggin, okay.

She quickly rearranges her hug into a pound. She then notices his sneakers.

Oh, what the fuck, those the Nike KDs?

Mr. Bugz   Yes, sir.

Val   Goddamn, they haven't even come out yet.

Mr. Bugz   Come on, you know me, Val, I get my shit prior to release.

Val   Lucky motherfucker. You see I'm rockin' my Tiffanys today.

Gerry   Can we save the fashion show for later?

Val   Ya'll gonna be down here?

Gerry (*as he enters the building*)   Where else they gonna be!

Lamont   He's on his period, so be careful.

Val *leans her Segway on the building.*

Val   Watch my shit.

She slips into the building following **Gerry**. **Bugz** *shakes his head, upset.* **Bugz** *and* **Lamont** *just chill for a second.*

Mr. Bugz   That man getting on my last nerve, yo.

Lamont   Gerry? Whatever, b, he always talkin' slick. That was nothin new.

Mr. Bugz   But I'm sayin, when we went and saw this musical, we get a drink after, right? And we actually have a conversation like two grown men, he starts opening up about when he used to be a millionaire—

Lamont   Gerry with a G?

Mr. Bugz   Yeah! He had some fuckin' paintbrush company or something, made all this money, but then fell into a deep depression when his friend Bob Ross died. So I'm like—

Lamont   Who?

Mr. Bugz   You don't know Bob Ross? The artist, you know, / the painter?

Lamont   Ohhhhh, that's my man with the fro, right?

Mr. Bugz   Yeah, happy little trees and shit, / you know.

Lamont   Right, right. Love that dude. Peaceful.

Mr. Bugz   *Very* peaceful. Well, Gerry and him were *boys*.

Lamont   Get the fuck outta here—

Mr. Bugz   *Yeah.* To tell you the truth I think Gerry was in love with him, but Bob Ross didn't fuck no dudes.

Lamont   Right.

Mr. Bugz   So when Gerry was talking about that, it somehow led to us talking about his relationship with his mother who *also* had Alzheimer's, you know what I'm saying—

Lamont   Ah, right.

Mr. Bugz   —and me and him basically went through a lotta the same shit, you know, moving our mom into a home, the guilt that comes with that—

Lamont   Right, right—

Mr. Bugz   —so I'm like, "Yo, this man is kinda deep, like we're actually having a good conversation right now." But then today he just goes off at the mouth as usual—

Lamont (*shaking his head*)   Psss, he ain't deep. He's blind. He's just as blind as the other 85 percent of the world, my brother, but whatever. That's just how it is.

The scene freezes. **Lamont** *raps to the audience.*

Arm, Leg, Leg, Arm Head, this God Body,
my truth of square where I stand, my squad by me,
we all righteous, the 10 percent fight us
and poison the 85ers with lies up in they attics
don't wanna see no addicts amongst my Asiatics,
that's why we study mathematics
try and reknit my culture's fabric
and get hit wit' automatics

Unfreeze. We shift focus up to **Gerry**'s *apartment. The place is a mess, clothes all over the floor.* **Gerry** *is searching through the pockets of several different pants, trying to find the wallet.*

Gerry   Goddamnit.

Val *enters from the bathroom.*

Val   So, Gerry with a G, I heard you and my man Bugz went to see some Broadway the other week?

Gerry   Uh-huh.

Val   That's cool.

Gerry   *No.* You want to know what's cool? *1959. That* was cool. When you had *Gypsy* and *The Sound of Music* opening in the same season. I mean, can you imagine? Can you even imagine? Ugh.

Val (*not really paying attention*)   Yeah, I feel that.

Gerry *continues to search.*

Gerry (*to himself*)   Oh, where the *hell* is my wallet?

Val   I been trying to tell you, man, just get Venmo.

Gerry   Get what?

Val   The thing I been telling you about. It's an app on your phone that lets you transfer money electronically.

Gerry   Ugh.

Val   You always losing your wallet so—

Gerry   Well, I'm also always losing my phone so what good does that do me?

Val (*chuckling*)   I think you also losing your mind, bro.

Gerry   Oh, I lost that back in May of 1977.

Val   Specific.

Gerry   Yup.

Val   What happened in May of 1977?

Gerry   *Star Wars*.

Val   You don't like *Star Wars*?

Gerry *turns to* **Val**. *Blows a large raspberry.*

Val *chuckles.*

Val   Yo, back when I first started interning at the radio station, there was this other intern named Anthony Something, and he was kinda tall and lanky, and you know me, I'm kinda Ms. Shorty McGee so Bugz used to call us C3PO and R2D2.

Gerry   So, Bugz is a fan of *Star Wars*, huh?

Val   I know he went to a convention when he was younger, but don't tell him I told you that.

Gerry   Really?

Val   Yeah, surprised me too.

Gerry   Well, lemme tell ya, sweetheart . . . there's uh . . . probably *a lot* of things about your friend Bugz that might surprise you.

Val   Like what?

Gerry *shoots her a look.*

Val   Like *what*?

Gerry   Let's just say that back in my day he's what we would refer to as a nance.

Val   A what?

Gerry   He's what my father would describe as being a little light in the loafers. He enjoys a little basket shoppin, if ya get what I mean. He's known to take a little trip over the bridge to Pimpleton.

Val   Yo, I ain't got a *clue* what you're talking about, yo.

Gerry   Alright, well, then lemme be a little more blunt for ya: when he closes his eyes, all he sees is *dick*.

Val   Ha. Right. You funny.

Gerry   You don't believe me.

Val   *Fuck* no.

Gerry   Okay.

Pause.

Val   You think he's *gay*?

Gerry *nods.*

Val   Well, what makes you think that?

Gerry *kinda shrugs, kinda nods, as if he just knows from his gut but doesn't have the words to say why.*

Val   You talkin' about a legend, you know that, right?

Gerry   Oh, please.

Val   No disrespect to you or nothin' but that's a strong ass accusation.

Gerry   No, sweetheart, saying someone is a racist is an accusation.

Val   You can't just—this man is one of the greatest DJs of all time, he about to be inducted into the hip-hop hall of fame.

Gerry (*condescending baby talk*)   Aw, he is? The hip-hop hall of fame? Aw, good for him. Aw, how cute, how special.

Val   Yo, you got my fuckin' money or what, I got shit I gotta do.

Gerry   Can you spot / me fifty—

Val   No, last time I spotted you it took you like a day a half to pay me back.

Gerry   Ugh.

Val   Just download the goddamn Venmo like I been telling you.

Gerry   YOU REALLY WANT AN ELECTRONIC TRACE OF A DRUG TRANSACTION?

Val   No one's gonna *know* it's a fucking drug transaction. Unless you write the reason in the payment section: "For cocaine."

Gerry (*taking out his phone*)   Oh, God, Jesus, alright, how the fuck do I do this?

Val   Go to the App Store.

A pause as **Gerry** *does this.*

Gerry   Now what.

Val   Type in Venmo.

Gerry   Vemmo?

Val   VEN-MO. V-e-n-m-o.

Gerry (*making fun of the word*)   Venmo. Vennnnnnnnnmo.

A pause as he slowly and exaggeratedly types with his pointer finger.

You know when I think this country took a wrong turn, Val? The Revolutionary War. We should have never separated from England, we shoulda just stayed under their rule like we belong, then everything would be much better.

Val   You got it?

Gerry   It says I gotta put in my Apple ID password.

Val   So put it in!

Gerry   WELL, HOW THE HELL AM I SUPPOSED TO KNOW WHAT THAT IS!

Val   How you don't know your own password?

Gerry   Oh, JESUS CHRIST! How many *passwords* do we *need* in this fucking world? You gotta have at least nine *letters*, and a *number* and an upper case Q and a fucking *question mark*—and then you have to *change* your password every other month for *security* reasons, ugh someone just kill me!

Val   Aight, for real though, what makes you think Bugz is gay? Just tell me.

Gerry (*half talking with his hands, can't fully articulate his thoughts*)   There's just a . . . you know he has that uh, uh, uh . . .

Val   You try and fuck him or something?

Gerry   *No.* Are you *kidding* me? I can just tell. It's a . . . it's a . . . I don't know how to explain it alright, but when you've been around as long as I have you start to—

Val (*clearly very upset*)   I can tell you for a fact that's he's not gay.

Pause.

Gerry   Look. I shouldn't have said anything. But that bastard's got a lot of nerve too, ya know! He called me a racist. And he was serious. And I was VERY offended by that.

Val   Why'd he call you that?

Gerry   Oh, 'cause I called a random black kid a thug.

Val (*quietly*)   There ya go.

Gerry   Big deal! BIG FUCKING DEAL! Jesus, everyone is so goddamn *sensitive* nowadays. What, because I called *one* black kid a thug, that means I think they all are? Because I referred to *one* kid—who was dancing in the middle of the goddamn subway, who almost *kicked* a little old lady in the head, who had *absolutely no regard* for anyone else on the subway, who when I politely asked to be careful he looked at me and said, "Fuck you, old man. I'll punch you in your motherfuckin' head, you fuckin' bitch!" Because I happened to—in a fit of rage—describe this *one* particular child in a way that didn't *sit well* with Bugz that means there's something wrong with me? That I'm a bigot? With everything going on in this world. With these fucking brutal cops and these evil, ignorant Republicans; *these lying monsters* trying to end our democracy . . . Bugz has the gall to lump me in with *those* assholes? After I take him to a show and we have a nice time? It's not right. It's just not right. I shouldn't have to *watch what I say*. I shouldn't have to bite my tongue, especially around friends.

Val   Friends?

Gerry   Yes, friends, believe it or not I actually consider those two bozos friends of mine. One's a closet case and one's homophobic, but FUCK IT! I still like them.

Val   So you got *no* money?

Gerry   You spot me fifty I'll pay you back a hundred dollars tonight. A hundred bucks! On my honor!

Val   Pssssss.

She hands **Gerry** *a bag of cocaine.*

Val   Pretty soon you gonna have to find another connect, aight, once the album is finished, I'm done with all this.

Gerry   Good for you. 'Cause I don't condone this stuff, you know. It's for someone else.

Val   Whatever.

Gerry   Cocaine is a terrible drug. It makes ya anxious, it makes ya ramble on and on—the amount of friends I used to have who sniffed half their salary up their nose is endless. It's an awful, awful drug, just despicable.

Val   It can be fun though.

Gerry   It can be a *lot* of fun.

He lights up a cigarette.

Val   You smoke in the house?

Gerry   Huh?

Val   I always thought you don't smoke in the house, that's why you're always downstairs.

Small pause. **Gerry** *receives a text.*

Gerry   Jesus Christ.

Val   What?

Gerry   One of my callers just broke the record for most money brought into the room in a week. She raised over a hundred and fifty thousand dollars.

Val   Well, that's a good thing, right?

Gerry   Yeah, it is . . . but now I just gotta . . . (*He sighs, exhausted by the idea of it.*) . . . now I gotta ask *Lamont* for a fucking favor.

Back to the stoop. **Bugz** *plays with a fidget spinner.*

Lamont   . . . just look at the fashion so-called rappers are rockin' these days. Skinny jeans. Rainbow hair. *Skirts*. These motherfuckas are actually rockin' skirts.

Mr. Bugz   I mean, men been rocking skirts for centuries in fuckin' um, Scotland.

Lamont   Yeah, and that's a Scottish thing, that's not a hip-hop thing. We're not talking about Scottish culture, we're talkin about *hip-hop* culture, and that's not hip-hop.

Val *enters.*

Lamont   People in hip-hop should not be wearing no skirts. But all of a sudden—even some of the harder rappers, even the ones that started out on some street, grimy style . . . now you see them more on some, you know, bohemian, hippie dippy shit, or some skinny jeans, glasses and a sweater vest kinda shit.

Val   Why you care so much about what people be wearing, God?

Lamont   I don't give a fuck what people wear. A man could walk around in a tutu if he wants. *I'm* just sayin', don't bring that shit into my culture, don't try and steer hip-hop into something that it's not.

Mr. Bugz   I agree.

Lamont   My man agrees.

Small pause.

Val   Yo, God, lemme ask you a question. You homophobic?

Lamont *shoots her a look.*

Lamont   Am I—where the fuck did that / come from?

Mr. Bugz   Yeah, why you asking that?

Val   The shit you say sometimes . . .

Lamont   The shit I say has absolutely nothin' to do with being homophobic.

Val   So you not?

Lamont   Look. Up in Harlem there's a saying I grew up with, "I don't care if you fuck guys or fuck girls, but don't you ever fuck me outta my money."

Bugz *laughs, him and* **Lamont** *give each other a pound.*

Lamont   And that's exactly how I feel.

Mr. Bugz   Likewise, bro.

Val (*to* **Lamont**)   You got any gay friends?

Lamont   Do I have any gay friends? Hmmm. Lemme think on that.

A long pause as he thinks.

Gerry *is at his window smoking, overhearing this conversation.*

Lamont (*an obvious realization*)   Oh! (*Now doubting that realization.*) Well . . .

Val   What?

Lamont (*gesturing up towards* **Gerry**'s *apartment*)   I mean, I guess you can kinda sorta call this—nah, nah never mind he ain't—

Val   Who, Gerry?

Lamont   Yeah, I mean he, you know, we kick it out here, but, a *friend*? Nah. (*To* **Bugz**.) Right? Gerry ain't our *friend*, is he?

Mr. Bugz (*thinking on it*)   Ehhhh. Nah. I don't think so.

Val   So you got *no* gay friends?

Lamont   I mean, there was some people that I grew up with that were definitely gay. I mean, not no close friends, but you know, in my periphery. And I'm sure there were *tons* of people that were, you know, closeted.

Mr. Bugz   Right.

Pause.

Yo, I'm a hit up the corner store. Ya'll need anything?

Lamont   Oh word, yeah, lemme get one of them veggie pasta joints they got laid out there.

Mr. Bugz   Val?

Val   I'm good.

Mr. Bugz *holds out his hand to* **Lamont** *for money*.

Lamont   I ain't got no more cash on me.

Mr. Bugz (*shaking his head*)   Psss. Whatever, just Venmo me later.

He exits down the block.

Val   Damn. Homie just skippity dipped his way up outta here.

Lamont   Yo, you listen to my nephew's album?

Val   Oh! Yeah, I did!

Lamont   Oh word?

Val   Shit is tight. I was gonna bring that up to you.

Lamont   The boy 'bout to be a problem, you don't even know.

Val   Bugz listen to it yet?

Lamont (*shaking his head*)   Psttt.

Val   I mean, you know, he's busy with his moms so . . .

Lamont   If he so busy, why the fuck he chillin' on this stoop every day?

Val (*laughing*)   True.

Lamont   He don't look that busy to me.

Val   I'm sayin' though, the stress.

Lamont   Yeah, whatever.

Pause.

You wanna bet ten dollars I can do ten pull-ups?

Val   You ain't got ten dollars.

Lamont *does the pull-ups. He can only do eight.*

Lamont   Damn. Getting old, Val. (*Pause.*) What the fuck is this holdin' out your hand shit like we in middle school?

Val   Huh?

Lamont   Bugz can't just front me, fuckin', six bucks or whatever that veggie pasta cost? How long I known him. And I don't fuck with that Venmo shit, I'm a cash in hand kinda man, always been.

Val   How long *have* you known Bugz?

Lamont   Shit, we're talking twenty-five, thirty years.

Val   And he always . . . been like he been?

Lamont   You mean *cheap*? Hell yeah. Motherfucker is a *miser*. Only thing he'll spend money is on that is that ridiculous sneaker collection. He's got about four hundred pairs a sneaks up there.

Val (*as if she thinks that's the coolest thing in the world*)   Ohhh, I knowwwww.

Lamont   Look, I love a fresh pair a kicks as much as the next man but four hundred? Come on, yo, that's just excessive.

Val   Nah, b, ain't no such thing.

Lamont   Ya'll two some sneaker junkies, I don't understand that shit.

Val   Yo, anyone that knows anything about being fly will tell you that when it comes to fashion? You dress from the feet up. And Bugz is one fly motherfucker. First time I even laid eyes on the man he was wearing the original—*original*—Nike Air Force. I'm talkin' from like 1982. And they were as white as a fuckin' albino, yo. I'm like, yo this man is a genius.

Lamont   A genius? Pss. Yo, people do not understand what that word means nowadays.

Small beat.

Val   You think Bugz been seeming like . . . I don't know, mad blue lately.

Lamont   Well, no shit, yeah, his moms is dying. And I feel for him, I really do, but we all got struggles, you know.

Val   It's a hard knock life, yo.

Lamont   A-ha, exactly, girl.

He puts on the instrumental for "Hard Knock Life" by Jay-Z. They bop to the music for a little.

Val   This the instrumental?

Lamont   Okay, I got something, I got something.

He starts to rap.

> Born Cipher—Knowledge Wisdom and Understandin'
> This Food4Thought will feed all the needy through
> the famine
> I've been to Japan and I've eaten their raw salmon
> Like the guards at Buckingham I'm always outstandin'
> My head's so big it could fill up the Grand Canyon
> I can send ya to the moon you can all me Ralph Cramden
> The business side of this business has got me bitter
> I'm sick a seeing these suckers instead of the raw spitters
> I listen to all these fibbers and I don't believe a word
> This mummble rap shit is the weakest I've ever heard
> I wanna take all that bullshit and kick it to the curb
> I don't wanna hear your story don't even read me the
> blurb
> The K-I-N-G never been trendy
> But the ride's still going, running on ten speed
> I can't describe the feeling these endorphins bring
> Now lemme pause and let these little orphans sing

Gerry *enters from the building, holding a small plastic bag. He plops a cigarette into his mouth. They all listen to the music.*

Gerry *(recognizing the beat)*   "Annie."

Lamont *nods.*

Lamont   Yup.

Gerry   I like this. Catchy.

Pause.

So, uh . . . would you mind turning that down a smidgen, I wanna talk to you about something. . . .

Lamont *turns off the music.*

Lamont   Sup?

Gerry *takes out a box of chocolates from his bag.*

Gerry   Would you like a Ferrero Rocher?

Lamont *looks at* **Gerry** *skeptically, but then takes a chocolate. He offers one to* **Val***. She also accepts.*

Gerry   So there's this girl that works for me—actually she's the best caller I have. Nancy. She's also a theater maker. Talented girl. Well, supposedly. I actually haven't seen anything of hers, and truthfully, chances are I'd despise it but *anyhoo*. I'm talking with my assistant and somehow I mention you and she turns to me and says, "Wait, are you talking about Lamont Born Cipher? From the group the uh uh uh—"

Val   Tha Enlightenuz.

Gerry   Whatever, yeah. So, I say, "I have no idea" 'cause I didn't. She googles you, I say, "Yup, that's him" . . . she freaks out. "You *know* him? You actually *know* this man, he is a legend, a LEGEND."

Val   He is.

Gerry   I say, "Really? Him? If he's such a legend why is he sittin' on my stoop every other day. Doesn't he have something better to do, something *legendary*." She says, "He is one of my *favorite* rappers of all time." I didn't even know you were an actual rapper, to be honest. (*Gesturing toward*

Bugz's *apartment*.) I mean, I knew about this one with the fun little, uh . . . (*Mimes a DJ scratching*.) . . . scratchy scratchy on the records, I knew about him and that highly respected art form . . . but I had no idea I was amongst *two* legends.

Lamont   Aight, so this chick knew of me, what of it?

Gerry   So on Monday I say to Nancy, to . . . you know, uh, incentivize her . . . I say, "You break the record this week, you raise more money in a single week then we've ever done before . . . and I will *introduce you* . . . to Lamont Born Cipher . . ."

Lamont   Oh, so you writing checks yo' ass can't cash . . .

Gerry (*confused*)   Huh?

Lamont (*answering his request*)   No.

Gerry   She's a sweet kid, you'll like her, you'll be doing me a huge favor.

Lamont   No.

Gerry   Come onnnn. She's from New York, she loves hip-hop, you two will get along just great.

Lamont   What part a New York she from?

Gerry   Scarsdale.

Lamont   No.

Gerry   Can ya / just—

Lamont   I'm not trying to chop it up with some little white girl just cause she's a fan, aight, I'm sorry, I don't got time for that.

Gerry   Whoever said she was white?

Beat.

Lamont   Well, is she?

Gerry   Well, yes, but you didn't know that.

Lamont   Nancy? I've met *very* few sisters in my life named Nancy, b.

Gerry   I fucked up, okay? I shoulda checked with you first, I apologize. But there was no way in hell I thought she'd ever break the record but she *did* . . . I made a bet and I lost. What kinda man would I be if I didn't follow through? (*Suddenly remembering.*) Ah! What is it . . . what is it I always hear ya saying, about your word . . .

Pause.

Lamont   My word is my bond.

Gerry   Well, so is mine. My word is my bond, Lamont. I *promised* her. Please.

Pause. **Lamont** *sighs.*

Val   Oh, using his own phrase against him, I like that, Gerry.

Gerry   Thank you.

Val (*rubbing* **Lamont***'s shoulders, teasing*)   Hoisted by your own petard, bro.

Lamont *sighs again heavily.*

Lamont   Lemme get another one of them chocolates.

Gerry *hands him the chocolate. He eats.*

Lamont   Aight, look. Tomorrow afternoon . . . at 3pm . . .

Gerry (*taking out phone, texting*)   Thank you.

Lamont   I will give this broad *ten minutes*!

Gerry   Thank you, whole thing will take two seconds.

Val   You a good dude, Lamont. Showing some love to the little white fans.

Lamont   Yeah, whatever.

Pause. **Lamont** *puts the music back on.* **Gerry** *finishes texting.*

Gerry (*small talk*)   So uh. You were a rapper, huh?

Lamont (*defensively*)   Still *am*.

Val   This man a legend.

Lamont   I mean, been puttin' that in the backseat lately, focusing on management.

Gerry   Managing your uh—

Lamont   My nephew, yeah. But I been inspired lately. Releasing a series of verses on YouTube. The Arm Leg Leg Arm Head series.

Gerry *politely nods. He has no idea what he's talking about. Small beat.*

Gerry   You know, to be honest I always kinda thought you were uh . . . that you were homeless. Was thinking about offering you my couch a couple times but we all know how that woulda turned out.

Lamont   Yeah, we all do. (*Shaking his head.*) Psst, homeless. Go fuck yourself, Gerry.

Mr. Bugz *comes back on. He's got his sandwich and a big jug of Gatorade. He hands the veggie dish to* **Lamont***.* **Gerry***, not wanting to engage with* **Bugz***, heads back into his building.*

Small pause.

Mr. Bugz   Yo, what you doing today, Val?

Val   You trying to get rid of me?

Mr. Bugz   Nah. Just asking. Damn. Touchy.

Bugz *starts eating his sandwich.*

Lamont   You know what, I actually think I'm gonna get up outta here.

Mr. Bugz   Where you going?

Lamont   What, you think I got no where else to be?

Mr. Bugz   I'm just asking. Goddamn, what the fuck is up with everyone today.

Lamont   I'll holler at you later, man, I'm just gonna eat this at home. Gotta go walk Selassie anyway.

Mr. Bugz   Aight, man, one.

Lamont *leaves*.

Bugz *is still eating*.

Mr. Bugz   Damn. Them Koreans make a mean sandwich, yo.

Val   Facts.

Another pause.

Yo, lemme ask you . . . would you consider yourself a selfish person?

A pause as **Bugz** *looks at her, very confused by where this is coming from.*

Mr. Bugz   I asked you if you wanted anything before I went to the store, didn't I?

Val   I mean, like, in general.

Mr. Bugz   What the fuck kinda question is that?

Val   Yo, my bad, b.

Bugz *continues to eat*.

Val   It's just—aight, don't tell him I told you. But Lamont mentioned to me you ain't listen to his nephew's album yet.

Mr. Bugz   I haven't listened to anything, Val. I mean, the thing with my job . . . I left my job at the station to take care of my dying mother, if I was in a listening-to-new-music mode, I'd still be working.

Val   Aight, yeah, true, true. (*Pause*.) But like. I remember I gave you a couple tracks that I recorded mad long ago. Like before your mother was diagnosed, and you ain't listen to that shit neither.

Mr. Bugz   Val. Do you know how many people want me to listen to their music? I mean, I'm sorry, yo, but I'm only human. You know I think you're nice. I told you when I heard you battling that dude with the big ears in the hallway.

Val   I don't think you realize how fuckin' difficult the industry is right now.

Mr. Bugz   I / do.

Val   Like these executives that I've met, these A and Rs . . . I feel like 90 percent of them were born with this rare condition that makes them gravitate towards music that is straight *ass*. Like I'm telling you, most these gatekeepers, they just love garbage, I don't get it—

Mr. Bugz   A lot of them don't know what they're doing, you right.

Val   And when you *pour your heart* into this shit every day. (*Brief beat*.) Like when I battled Big Ears McGee in the hallway, that was just some off the head bullshit. The shit I sent you was like . . . personal.

Bugz *puts his sandwich aside*.

Mr. Bugz   Aight, aight. Lemme hear that shit right now.

Val (*taking her phone out*)   Word. I got it right here.

Mr. Bugz   Nah, nah, I'm sayin, spit it, girl! You a rapper, right, rap that shit.

Val   With no beat?

Mr. Bugz *beatboxes for her. She hesitates a little.*

Val   Yo, yo, check it, yo, yo, check it, check it, check it, yo . . .

Then she begins to rap.

Val

They call me super fly chica,
a bad ass Boricua,
studded from the top of my dome down to my sneakas,
I'm quick to pick a bitch apart critique ya like a teacher,
flowin' like the Nile while smilin' like the Mona Lisa,
I'm leanin' like the Pisa,
Always pack a piece
Discover how I stick ya for your Amex, Mastercard, or Visa,
Hailing from the slum
but still got the spirit of Big, Pac, and Pun
all rolled into one
Lay my heart on the line every since my father died
Committed to killin' the kid that did the homicide
see them both in my eyes when I look into the mirror,
Now that's three killas all addicted to the skrilla
Every man I ever met
showed me disrespect
so when I cut off their dick you better bet / they're gonna
get—

Bugz *starts coughing.*

Mr. Bugz (*through his cough*)　Damn, shit is hot, yo, that verse is tight for real. Sorry, man, just choked on my spit a little bit.

Val　You were feelin' it though?

Mr. Bugz　That last part surprised me, but yeah, it was good. *Fuck* you're talented as hell, Val. You need to just keep on rapping, that's all. And battling too, you know, you got a naturally aggressive nature to you, I like that.

Val　Oh yeah?

Mr. Bugz　Don't let these stupid A and Rs get you down. Shit just takes a while, trust me, that's how it is. And I feel like now's the time for female emcees too, everywhere I look there's more and more poppin' out the woodwork.

Val   Well, thank you.

Mr. Bugz   You're welcome.

Pause. **Val** *smiles, genuinely touched.*

Val   I miss chillin' with you, yo.

Mr. Bugz   Don't we chill like almost every other day?

Val   I know, but . . . yeah. (*Small pause.*) So, when things get better suited with your moms, you headed back to the station?

Mr. Bugz   Yup.

Val   Guess who I'm grabbing dinner with later on tonight? Charlie O.

Mr. Bugz   Oh yeah? Tell that moron I said "What up."

Val *laughs.*

Val   How's Goran?

Mr. Bugz   Same ol', breath still kickin'.

Val   Oh my God, that breath is lethal, yo, I swear.

Mr. Bugz   Why is it that the people with the stankiest breath are also the closest talkers?

Val   I don't know, but that's true, it's like a weird correlation.

Mr. Bugz   I'm like, "Yo, Goran, I could talk to you from over here, you ain't gotta keep inchin' forward."

Val   Word, yo, word.

Mr. Bugz   That place is crazy, yo. Every other—

Val   Yo, can I ask you . . . back when I used to give you head how come you never reciprocated?

Pause.

Mr. Bugz   Uhhh—

Val   I've always wondered, and you know, we never really talked about it.

Mr. Bugz   I mean, I don't . . . you never asked?

Pause. **Val** *sighs.*

Mr. Bugz   I mean, that one time I was about to but you were on your period . . . (*Pause.*) Why you bringing this up now?

Val *shrugs.*

Val   Do you not like eating pussy?

Mr. Bugz   Nah, yo, I love it. I don't know, we just, uh . . . I mean . . . I just . . . you know, like . . . I mean . . . I *woulda* if . . .

Val   I'm not mad or anything like—I'm just curious.

Mr. Bugz   I uh. I mean, I woulda done it if you asked me. Simple as that, yo, but I mean—yo why are we talking about this?

Val   It was just on my mind.

Mr. Bugz   You pissed that I never listened to your tracks? That it?

Pause.

Val   Is it cause you didn't feel intimacy with me?

Mr. Bugz   I just told you, I woulda—

Val   I don't understand you sometimes, Bugz. It's like—I got the impression that we were done with all that. But then . . . you be texting me at four in the morning. Just like . . . "What up."

Mr. Bugz   Yeah I know.

Val   And I'm like, "Nothin', what up with you, you wanna chill?"

Mr. Bugz   Uh-huh.

Val   But then you're like . . ."Nah, I just wanna talk." So I'm like . . .

She makes a "I'm confused" face.

Mr. Bugz   You don't like just talking sometimes?

Val   At four in the morning? I mean, yeah I do, but that makes me think that like—I don't know—there's maybe more to this then—whatever I'm making no sense. (*Pause.*) So then that one time I'm like, "Aight, what you wanna talk about?" And you just go, "Nothing." Like . . . you got me mad baffled.

Mr. Bugz   I was just sayin' . . . it's nice, I don't know, being in contact with you still, that's all . . .

Val   So you're saying you want more than . . .

Mr. Bugz   I'm not sayin' nothing, I'm just sayin'.

Pause.

Val   Are you mad blue lately?

Mr. Bugz   Of course I'm blue. My moms is dying, yo.

Val   But I mean . . . (*Slight beat.*) Do you wanna still . . . *hang out* hang out or nah?

Mr. Bugz   We do hang out.

Val *shakes her head, frustrated.*

Gerry *enters holding his wallet.*

Gerry   Found my wallet. The sheets. The goddamn tangled sheets.

He hands her a hundred bucks.

Gerry   A hundred *bones*, as promised.

Pause.

Well. I'm off to work.

Mr. Bugz   Ya'll have a good day. I'll talk to you later, Val.

He exits into the building.

Pause.

Gerry   I could hear ya, uh . . . (*Starts doing over the top rap hands.*) . . . doing some rippity rippity from the window. Little rippity rappity roo. (*Rapping, pretending to be her.*)

> Yeah, my name is Val
> and I'm the best,
> I'm the best,
> I'm the best.

Tell me that's not every fucking rap song you've ever heard in your life.

Val   Why you always gotta be a dick, Gerry?

Gerry   'Cause I'm real, that's why.

Transition: **Lamont** *enters and raps to the audience.*

Lamont
> Arm Leg Leg Arm Head, this God Body
> My Truth of Square where I stand
> My Squad By Me
> I stay righteous
> But they don't want righteous
> They wanna hand me another knife to fight with
> They wanna change my likeness
> They want Zeus,
> they don't want Osiris
> They short sighted
> They say "Bring more violence"
> But shrug when I bring my people more kindness
> It's why I keep that go-to-war mindset

We segue to later on that night. The music from the rap fades out and turns into Cole Porter's "Anything Goes" coming from **Gerry***'s record player.*

Bugz *knocks on* **Gerry***'s door.*

Mr. Bugz   Yo, Gerry. It's Bugz.

Gerry *opens the door.*

Gerry   Music too loud?

Mr. Bugz   Nah. Can I come in?

He enters.

Mr. Bugz (*re: the music*)   Who is this?

Gerry   Cole Porter. Now *that* man could rhyme. Not like the trash you and your friend are always listening to. Half of it doesn't even rhyme. "Dr*eam*, maga*zine*." That's just lazy.

Mr. Bugz   Sometimes it ain't about the rhymes but what they're saying.

Gerry   Oh, 'cause what they're saying is sooooooo deep. The *scope*. The scope of what these gentlemen have to say is so incredibly vast.

Mr. Bugz   Yo man, I don't wanna—(*Slight beat.*) I actually came over to apologize.

Gerry *waits.*

Mr. Bugz   I feel like I attacked you earlier. When I called you a racist. I don't think you're a racist. (*Small beat.*) But I do think sometimes you say racist shit.

Gerry   To say that I don't *respect* poor / black people—

Mr. Bugz   Well, the language you use—

Gerry   If anything I don't respect *rich* black people. I don't respect rich people period. When I was a millionaire I did everything I could to lose all my money. I would go to the bar and pay for everyone. Black, white, brown, men, women, whatever. I thought I was gonna be dead soon anyway so who gives a shit.

Mr. Bugz   Yeah, I know, you a . . . you a generous person, ain't no one denying that. (*Pause.*) Well, anyway, I definitely snapped at ya, man, and I'm uh, I'm sorry about that.

Pause.

Gerry   Would you like some marijuana?

Another beat.

Mr. Bugz   Aight.

Gerry *lights up a bowl. Puff puff pass.*

Mr. Bugz   Was thinking about the musical we saw.

Gerry   Ugh. *Why?*

Mr. Bugz   I just remember sitting there being like, "Man, this shit is aight." I mean, it was *corny*, don't get me wrong. But I found myself . . . I don't know. Then I look around, I'm like, "Goddamn, I am the only black person up in this place." Made me feel like . . . (*He shrugs; pause.*) The next morning I went to my old neighborhood in Bed Stuy.

There was this little kid sittin' on a stoop, right. Adorable little kid, wearing a bow tie. And he's playing with this rubick's cube trying to figure it out. So, I notice him, right. Park my car, take a stroll, just, you know, walking around, wandering basically. I come back, shit, musta been an hour and a half later. Little man is still playing with this rubick's. I'm thinking, "Damn, this kid *can not* figure this thing out." He kept trying though, like mad, you know, diligent.

Gerry   Good for him. I like hearing that. Nowadays kids are so goddamn distracted, with the i-Phones and the Facebook, and the this and the that . . . it's good to see that our youth are still capable of—

Bugz *immediately starts sobbing. It's out of nowhere.* **Gerry** *isn't sure how to deal with it.*

Mr. Bugz   I'm sorry. I'm sorry, man. I'm sorry. It's just . . . it's just . . . (*He takes another huge breath.*) . . . shit with my mom, ya know. It's just shit with my . . .

Another pause as he weeps.

Oh my God, this is so fucking embarrassing.

Gerry   Don't uh. Don't worry about it.

Long pause. **Bugz** *controls himself. Takes a breath.*

Mr. Bugz   Sorry.

Another pause.

Gerry   God, I couldn't wait for my mother to die. I could not wait. Then of course I felt all the guilt for feeling that way. I thought I must be the worst person to ever exist. I thought I'm just gonna go to a priest and admit what an awful, despicable person I am.

Mr. Bugz   And did you go?

Gerry   No, of course not.

Mr. Bugz   Yeah, you don't . . . you don't strike me as a religious.

Gerry   Well, the church's views on . . .

He makes a gesture, implying "homosexuality."

Mr. Bugz   Can I ask you, did you always know you were gay?

Gerry   Bugz . . . I am not gay. I am what you call a bisexual.

Mr. Bugz   Nah . . .

Gerry   Yes. Granted I haven't slept with a woman in—but still.

Mr. Bugz   So you like pussy, huh?

Gerry   I like everything.

Mr. Bugz   You like *everything*?

Gerry   I like a lot of things. I find myself akin to the Romans, Mr. Bugz. You know about the Romans?

Mr. Bugz I know that they stole from the Greeks who stole from the Egyptians.

Gerry That's not—anyway. Regarding sex. Sexuality. Let's just say the Romans were a lot less repressed than our society is today in America.

Mr. Bugz Less repressed how?

Gerry Freer.

Mr. Bugz So, what, everyone was just out in the streets, fucking each other?

Gerry Well, prostitution was legal—not only legal, but promoted. The literature, the art—even the epitaphs on the tombstones, they were all filled with *fucking*. And why? Because these wants and needs and desires are natural. No matter how depraved they are. It's these fucking *rules* in society that—you know I can talk about this all night, these are all issues I plan to grapple with in the musical I'm gonna write and produce one day about the life of Augustus, Rome's first emperor.

Mr. Bugz I didn't know you were a writer.

Gerry You don't see shows like this nowadays, Bugz, ya just don't. Everything is so *small*. What I wanna do is . . . (*Makes a gesture of a small circle with his hands and then expands it outward.*) . . . *grand*. Big, *big* shows, big issues, I'm talking *South Pacific, Sweeney Todd*, *these* were shows that—oh, you don't care.

Mr. Bugz Nah, I care. I feel you, bro, I *feel* you.

Pause. **Gerry** *can tell that* **Bugz** *is legitimately interested. He continues.*

Gerry I've got the whole first scene mapped out in my head. The curtain will rise on the forum, circa September, 27 BC. It'll be in the round, of course. The stage will be bare. Then one by one members of the senate will slowly approach from the audience. Dressed in togas, naturally. No music, yet. Just a faint drum. (*As he taps on his lap.*) "*Bum bum bum, bum bum bum bum bum, bum bum bum.*" Then once all the senators are on stage—this can take as long as it needs to, we're in for a three-hour evening anyway—once they're all on stage they turn to the audience, (*kind of singing*) "Augustus! Where is Augustus?" And that's when the trumpets come in, obviously. "Augustus! We need Augustus." Now this'll be late in Augustus' life, see. And one by one, through a series of verses by the senate, we will learn that today is the day Augustus is due to announce his heir to the throne, which of course ends up being Gaius.

And when Augustus finally arrives, he will sing to the audience—in what I imagine a celestial tenor—his fear of all his heirs being killed before him, and dying with the knowledge that the next emperor of Rome will be one whom he doesn't trust.

> Who will succeed me?
> Who will be my heir?
> Rome, she doth need me.
> Don't leave her in dispair

Something like that. This soliloquy will prove to be quite prophetic, of course, since Gauis and then later Luicuis are murdered and the next emperor of Rome become Tiberius, who Augustus can't stand. But that all comes later during the 11 o'clock number. "Augustus! All hail Augustus!"

Pause.

Gerry   Look, this all may sound dumb, with me telling it to you here in my living room, stoned out of my mind, but I'm telling you with the lights, and the music and the cosutmes . . . ah . . . it'll be magical.

Mr. Bugz   It don't sound dumb. Sounds pretty epic to tell you the truth.

Pause.

Gerry   Anyway . . . one of these days I'll get around to writing it.

Mr. Bugz   I don't know, man.

Gerry   What don't you know?

Mr. Bugz   I'm just saying, if you write that shit, it's prolly gonna be a big hit cause it sounds genius, and you gonna be a famous Broadway writer or whatever, and you know, with fame comes, with fame comes, what's the word I'm looking—

Gerry   Responsibility.

Mr. Bugz   Well, that too, but nah. Scrutiny. Trust me, yo. With fame comes scrutiny.

Gerry   Yeah, well . . . sometimes it'd be nice to be paid attention to.

Small beat.

Mr. Bugz   Yo, real talk, how did your boy Bob Ross remain so peaceful? I mean, he was a celebrity. He had his show, how did he not just . . . you know.

Gerry (*with a sad sense of nostalgia*)   Well. He was a remarkable man. (*Small beat.*) And he loved his whiskey. Could drink anyone under the table.

Mr. Bugz   We all got our vices, right? (*Takes another huge breath.*) Sometimes I just wish I could take my head and throw it off my shoulders.

Pause.

Gerry   Maybe uh. You got too much time on your hands. Maybe going back to work is a good idea.

Mr. Bugz   But my moms, man, she needs a lot of care these days.

Gerry   Yeah, well, Bugz, you're not exactly—no offense— you're not exactly at her bedside full-time now, are ya?

Unless she's got a bed next to that stoop that I don't know about. I think going back to the station would be good for you.

Mr. Bugz   Look, man, I didn't take a leave of absence cause a my moms, aright? They asked me to uh . . . take a little break.

Gerry   Why?

Pause.

Okay.

Pause. **Bugz** *takes another breath.*

Mr. Bugz   I'm going back to work on Monday. And I got a big decision I gotta make. A big, big decision.

He takes another huge breath. Exhales.

They want to interview me . . . on the air . . . and ask me some uh . . . questions . . . about certain illicit activities. That I may or may not have been partaking in.

Gerry   What kind of illicit activities?

Another pause.

Mr. Bugz   I'm just worried about my family. My sisters, my aunts and uncles . . . my mother. I don't want them to . . . and my fans . . . I don't want them to . . . view me differently.

Gerry *gives him a comforting squeeze on the shoulder.*

Gerry   You'll be alright. The Queen was ninety-six years old. Just remember that.

Pause. **Bugz** *feels safe, comfortable; makes a decision.*

Mr. Bugz   Aight, fuck it, tell me.

Gerry   Tell you what?

Mr. Bugz   Tell me about the erotic dream you had.

Another pause.

Gerry   Would you like something to drink?

Mr. Bugz   What you got?

Gerry *gets up, goes to the liquor.*

Gerry   Let's see here. Templeton Rye, 'bout a half a bottle left. An eighteen-year-old Glenlivet. And Laphroaig.

Mr. Bugz   I'll have whatever you having.

Gerry *pours two glasses. They cheers.*

Gerry   Salud.

Mr. Bugz   L'chaim.

They drink.

Gerry   Not bad, huh?

Mr. Bugz   Taste great.

Gerry   Little whiskey, little marijuana . . . little Cole Porter. My kinda evening.

Mr. Bugz   Yup.

Another pause.

Gerry   So . . . you wanna know about this dream . . .

Mr. Bugz   I'm just curious.

Gerry   You're not gonna get all . . .

Mr. Bugz   I'm fine, yo, I'm high, I'm chillin', I'm good.

Gerry   Okay. (*Pause.*) It had to do with your legs.

Mr. Bugz   My legs?

Gerry   I think I may be very attracted to your legs.

Mr. Bugz   Really?

Gerry   And by think I mean I am. I am 100 percent cognitive of that fact that I am attracted your legs.

Mr. Bugz *kind of laughs*.

Gerry (*shrugging*)   I like legs, what do ya want me to tell ya? Calves, in particular.

Mr. Bugz   Aight. So . . . what about 'em . . .

Gerry   Well, your calves, in the dream were kinda pumping outward and inward. Like a heart.

Mr. Bugz   Aight.

Gerry   Ya know, like you were flexing your calf muscles.

Mr. Bugz   Yeah, I got ya. And?

Gerry   And that's it.

Mr. Bugz   That's it?

Gerry   Well, that's all I remember.

Mr. Bugz   That's *it*?

Gerry   Well, I was very aroused by this, but yeah, that's it.

Mr. Bugz   So, you didn't do nothing? In the dream?

Gerry   Nope. I woke up.

Pause. **Mr. Bugz** *feels his own legs*.

Mr. Bugz   I guess I do got nice legs, huh?

Gerry   They're not bad.

They stare at each other for a long time. **Gerry** *takes another big swig of his drink. Then he gets up and slowly goes over to where* **Bugz** *is sitting.* **Bugz** *has his legs spread out.* **Gerry** *slowly gets down on his knees and starts to feel* **Bugz**'*s thighs. He moves his hand down to* **Bugz**'*s knee and then to his calf.* **Bugz** *just lets it happen.*

Gerry *then puts his other hand on* **Bugz**'s *other leg. Feels that one as well.*

Bugz *gently puts his hand on top of* **Gerry**'s *head.*

Then he forcibly pushes **Gerry**'s *head down into his crotch, jerking his neck way too roughly.*

Gerry   Ow, Jesus—

Mr. Bugz   I'm sorry.

Gerry *gets up and grabs his neck in pain.*

Gerry   Ow.

Mr. Bugz   That hurt?

Gerry (*holding his neck*)   Esssh. Yeah.

Mr. Bugz   Shit, I'm sorry, I thought—

Gerry   No, it's—you just gotta—

Mr. Bugz   I'm sorry.

Pause.

Gerry   I'm an old man, ya know, ya can't just—

He makes an aggressive pushing gesture.

Mr. Bugz   I'm sorry. Jesus, I'm sorry, Gerry.

A long, awkward pause.

I should uh. . . . probably get up outta here.

He gets up.

I really did not mean to hurt you, Gerry. I feel terrible.

Gerry   Mr. Bugz, there's plenty of things in this world to feel terrible about, that's not one of them.

Mr. Bugz   Aight. I know this goes without saying. . . . but can we . . .

Gerry   No, I'm gonna tell everyone. I'm gonna broadcast it to the whole neighborhood. I'm gonna write about it on the uh, the uh . . . on my Twitter.

Mr. Bugz   Aight. Have a good night, man. Again, I'm real s—

He stops himself from saying sorry. Then exits. **Gerry** *sits down and rubs his neck.*

Act Two

The next day. **Gerry** *is in his apartment with* **Nancy Reinstein**, *twenties. As usual he's looking for something.*

Gerry   Now, don't embarrass me.

Nancy   I won't.

Gerry   I mean it now, just . . . don't say anything stupid.

Nancy   Scout's honor.

Gerry   This man is a friend, okay? He's my boy. You know my uh . . . my homie. So just . . . don't embarrass me.

Nancy   I'm not gonna embarrass you. Can we go?

Gerry   And just . . . make it quick, okay, don't talk his ear off.

Nancy   I appreciate you doing this, G. Seriously, it means a lot.

Gerry   Well . . . just . . . don't embarrass me.

Nancy   What are you looking for?

Gerry   My mind! I'm looking for my mind.

Shift focus downstairs. **Bugz** *and* **Lamont** *chill.* **Lamont** *checks his watch.*

Lamont   How the fuck am I doing this man a favor and *I'm* the one that's early? Goddamn, yo.

Bugz *just kinda chuckles to himself, very distracted.*

Lamont   You aight, man?

Mr. Bugz   Huh?

Lamont   Just checking in with you, that's all. You seem distracted lately.

Mr. Bugz   Yeah, man, I'm good. Just . . . my moms, ya know?

Back upstairs.

Nancy   Okay, one gotta go . . . If you *had to* . . . get rid one of these four from existence, who would it be?

Gerry   I fucking hate this game, alright go.

Nancy   You love it. Okay, one gotta go: Jerome Kern. Richard Rodgers. George Gershwin. Stephen Sondheim.

Gerry   I'm not playing.

Nancy   Come on.

Gerry   No, fuck you.

Shift back downstairs.

Lamont   You know you my man, right?

Mr. Bugz   Nah, you my man.

Lamont   Nah, you *my* man.

Mr. Bugz   Nah you my man.

Lamont   Son, you my man.

Mr. Bugz   You *my* man!

They give each other a pound.

Mr. Bugz   You *been* my man, dawg, for what, twenty-five, thirty years?

Lamont   Shit, since what, the RUN-DMC tour in '89!

Mr. Bugz   Best group of all time.

Lamont   I mean, I might have to throw the Juice Crew up there—

Mr. Bugz   Where you rank the Furious Five?

Lamont   Okay, well if we talking back in the *days* back in the days . . . I'm going with the Cold Crush brothers cuz you know Caz is my favorite ever.

Mr. Bugz Cold Crush over Furious Five? You crazy!

Lamont My preference, my personal preference.

Shift back up.

Nancy The *point* of the game is to be hard, G. I know they're all great, but if you *had to* get rid of one, who would it be? (*Small beat as* **Gerry** *thinks.*) I mean, I know it'd be a lot easier if I said Kern, Rodgers, Gershwin and Andrew Lloyd Webber—

Gerry Oh, Webber's gotta go—

Nancy I know—

Gerry (*mimes picking up a soccer ball and kicking it*) Pick him up, boot him right outta here.

Nancy I know, but what's interesting about that? It's *supposed* to be a difficult choice, that's what's fun about it.

Gerry Ugghhh.

Shift back down.

Mr. Bugz I got NWA as my number two.

Lamont Over Public Enemy? Are you stupid? Are you actually stupid? And you from New York, what's wrong with you?

Mr. Bugz My preference, yo, my personal preference

Shift back up.

Nancy Rodgers?

Gerry Are you out of your mind? Rodgers is going nowhere.

Nancy Gershwin?

Gerry You can't rid of Gershwin.

Nancy Then Kern?

Gerry   Jerome Kern wrote "Ol' Man River"!

Nancy   So then it's Sondheim.

Gerry   I will slap you right now.

Shift back down.

Lamont   Rakim came *before* Nas so how the fuck you / have Nas over Rakim?

Mr. Bugz   I'm sayin', I'm sayin', I think Nas is nicer, it's no disrespect to Ra but—

Lamont   That is blasphemy, dawg, that is actual blasphemy.

Shift back up.

Gerry   This game is ridiculous! See, now, Rogers and Sondheim are my two favorites but you can't get rid of Gershwin or Kern because they came first and had a significant influence on the other two. That's what used to happen in the old days, artists would influence each other while still maintaining what the art form was meant to be. Instead of, you know . . . just bringing in some electric guitars and playing loudly.

Shift back down.

Lamont   I guess you never heard of a man by the name of Melle Mel.

Mr. Bugz   Motherfucker, I was at Melle Mel's wedding.

Lamont   Then why am I not hearing *his* name in your top five?

Shift back up.

Gerry   Okay, if I *had* to say. If my *life* depended on it I guess I would get rid of . . .

A couple moments as his face shifts into excruciating pain, as if it's physically difficult to say what he's about to say.

Gershwin.

He immediately covers his mouth, appalled at himself.

Nancy   Yeah, me too.

Shift back down.

Mr. Bugz   It's been a long ass time, dawg.

Lamont   For real. And I just want you to know that . . . I understand now is a hard time for you. I get that. Believe me I do. My aunt who passed away, she had dementia. I mean, granted I wasn't that close with her, but you know, I can understand what that might do to a brother's psyche. Seeing a loved one go through that. No one should have to do that. It ain't right.

Mr. Bugz   Nah, it ain't.

Lamont   And when people are faced with struggle, trauma, all that . . . (*Pointing to his head.*) . . . that's when the devil really gets in. Ya nah'mean? (*Pointing to his heart.*) That's why you gotta be strong here.

Mr. Bugz   I've done some devilish things.

Lamont   We all have, b. But you ain't no devil. You *God.* You know that, right? You already *are* God, my brother. You are the original man; the Asiatic Black man; the Maker, the Owner, the Cream of the planet Earth—Father of Civilization, God of the Universe. That's *you.* Can't nobody change that.

They give each other a heartfelt pound. **Lamont** *checks his watch.*

Lamont   Yo, this is ridiculous, I'm a go get a six pack. I need to have at least a little buzz to deal with this shit.

Mr. Bugz   Oh remember you owe me seven bucks. For that veggies pasta yesterday.

Small pause.

Lamont   Aight. Yeah.

He starts to leave . . .

Mr. Bugz   Yo. I'm fuckin' with you, bruh. Don't sweat it.

Shift back up.

Nancy   Hey, G. If they ever made a *Star Wars* musical on Broadway what would you do?

Gerry *gives her a disgusted look.*

Gerry   Stop talking to me.

Nancy   Sorry.

Gerry *finds what he's been looking for. It's* **Mr. Bugz***'s spinner. He spins it on his finger.*

Nancy   Stressed?

Gerry   Always. Let's go.

They head downstairs.

Gerry   Hello, Mr. Bugz.

Mr. Bugz   Gerry.

Gerry (*handing* **Bugz** *the spinner*)   You left this last night. Found it in my cushion then misplaced it and found it again. My apartment is like a fucking black hole.

Mr. Bugz   That's not mine.

Small pause.

Gerry   O-kay.

He puts the spinner back in his pocket.

This is one of my callers, Nancy.

Mr. Bugz   What's up?

Nancy   We've actually talked before. On the phone. I tried to sell you some tickets and you told me—albeit very politely—to go fuck myself.

Mr. Bugz (*looking at* **Gerry***, pointing at* **Nancy**)   I told you.

Gerry (*to* **Nancy**)   How did you get his number?

Nancy   What do you mean? His lead was on my desk.

Gerry   But I never—he never even purchased—this is very confusing.

Nancy   I'm a big fan of yours by the way.

Mr. Bugz   Thank you.

Nancy   I would actually go as far as to say that you're my favorite DJ of all time—

Mr. Bugz   That's very nice—

Nancy   —right behind Premier, Jam Master Jay, and Kid Capri. So you're my *fourth*, my fourth favorite DJ in the history of hip-hop.

Gerry   Easy now, Nancy.

Mr. Bugz (*chuckling*)   That's still—that's still a huge honor. I'm in good company.

Nancy   So you're like . . . really good friends with Lamont Born Cipher?

Mr. Bugz   Yup.

Nancy   Awesome.

Mr. Bugz   Uh-huh.

Nancy   Is it true he's completely broke?

Gerry   Hey, Nancy . . .

Mr. Bugz   What?

Nancy   I'm sorry, I don't mean to—I'm on these chat rooms all the time, Rap Grid dot com, things like that—

Gerry   That's none of your business.

Nancy   I'm just confused. Tha Enlightnuz were on top of the world in the Nineties.

Mr. Bugz   The Nineties were a long ass time ago.

Nancy   But *Out Tha Gate* went gold, how—

Gerry   *I* used to be a millionaire, ya know. Things change.

Val *enters on her Segway.*

Gerry   Ah. Val, this is one of my callers, Nancy. Nancy, this is my drug dealer Val. Oh, and you both like to rippity rap, so you know . . .

He makes a vague gesture with his hands of the two of them coming together and becoming friends. Whatever that is.

Val   Oh, you rhyme?

Nancy   I do indeed.

Val   Word?

Nancy   Uh-huh.

Val   That's cool.

Mr. Bugz   Val is a *beast*.

Val   What you mean I'm a *beast*?

Mr. Bugz   I mean . . . you're nice. You're a beast on the mic. The fuck you think I mean?

Nancy   I actually have a show opening if you guys are interested.

Gerry   But you're not obligated.

Val   What show?

Nancy   Well, it's about . . .

Lamont *enters with the beers.*

Gerry   Uhp, well, here he is. Lamont. This is Nancy.

Lamont   What's going on?

They shake hands.

Nancy   Hey I am—wow. I am a huge huge huge fan.

Lamont   Thank you. There's beer here if anyone wants . . .

He places the bag by the stoop. Takes out a can and pops it.

Nancy   I was telling G earlier . . . that *Out Tha Gate* . . . that album . . . changed my life.

Lamont   Say word.

Mr. Bugz   Yeah, *Out Tha Gate* changed a lotta lives.

Val   Facts.

Lamont   Yeah, it was a dope album.

Nancy   Oh, the dopest. Without a doubt.

Val   What's your favorite song on there?

Nancy   Oh, man. Too many to name. But gun to my head? I'd probably say . . . "Truth of Square"?

Val   Fire song.

Lamont   Yup.

Nancy (*quoting the lyrics*)   "My words soak into my journal, hot like an inferno, I'm the colonel of this rap shit, fuck a delivery, my flow is straight DiGiorno."

Mr. Bugz   Woo, hell yeah!

Val   Shit is fire.

Gerry   I don't get it.

Mr. Bugz   This girl knows her rhymes.

Lamont   No doubt. I mean . . . that wasn't one of *my* rhymes—

Nancy   Oh, I know—

Lamont   That was / Strictly B—

Nancy   That's a Strictly B lyric, yeah, I was just saying as an example from that song—

Lamont   Nah, it's cool, don't sweat it. Strictly B is a gifted lyricist.

Nancy   You guys still tight?

Lamont   Nope.

He takes a swig of his beer. Pause. **Nancy** *waits for* **Lamont** *to elaborate. He doesn't.*

Mr. Bugz   So who else you like, Nancy?

Nancy   Man . . . (*Looking at her watch.*) How much time do you have?

Mr. Bugz   You like Eminem?

Nancy   Eminem is a genius. He is a bona fide genius.

Mr. Bugz   I agree.

Lamont   He's very talented.

Gerry   You know I listened to an Eminem song once. Gave me a splitting headache.

Lamont *chuckles.*

Nancy   Yeah, well, you're just a hater, G.

Gerry   You all know my opinion when it comes to rap music. You all know that I . . . *loathe* it from the very bottom of my heart . . .

Mr. Bugz   Yup, we do.

Gerry   But I gotta say . . . I especially hate it . . . I *especially* hate it when white people are doing it.

Lamont   Oh, okay, this is interesting . . .

Gerry   It looks stupid. I'm sorry, but it's true. I said it. It just looks stupid. Do white people really have to try and *rap*? Really? Really? *Reallllllly?* I mean, black people have so little in this country, can't we just let them have that?

Lamont   Damn, Gerry, you keep it real as a motherfucka, you know that?

Gerry   *Yes I do.*

Val   Ignore him, yo. What were you sayin' . . . about a show you got coming up?

Nancy   Oh, yeah, it's a show I wrote and I'm starring in—Gerry is coming tonight—

Gerry   And hey, if I like it, I like it. I've been wrong in the past and when I am I *always* admit it.

Nancy   You're gonna hate it.

Gerry   Most likely.

Nancy   But anyway. It's a hip-hop musical all about the life of Amelia Earhart.

Mr. Bugz   Oh word?

Nancy   Yeah. I been working on it for a while now. My hope is that it's gonna be the first ever *feminist* hip-hop musical. And who better than Amelia Earheart, right? I mean, she was the first woman to ever fly, and think abut the word fly, you know, it's like there's fly and then there's (*Makes gesture indicating to look good.*) . . . *fly*, you know, it's such a—

Mr. Bugz   "Flyer than the piece of paper bearing my name—"

Nancy   "Got the hottest chick in the game wearing my chain" exactly!

Mr. Bugz   That sounds dope.

Nancy   You guys wanna hear a little snippet?

Gerry   Easy now, Nancy.

Nancy   If you don't want to it's totally cool, I don't wanna waste your time—

Val   Spit that shit.

Nancy   It'd just be . . . an honor . . . to rap in front of you in particular, Lamont.

Small pause.

Mr. Bugz   Let the girl rap, Lamont!

Lamont   I didn't even say anything yet, goddamn. Aight, let's hear it.

Gerry   Jesus Christ.

Nancy   Just a snippet, G, I promise. This is from a song called 'Take Flight'. Alright, here we go.

She gets in the zone, starts to rap.

> Yo, they called my mom Amy,
> my dad named Edwin
> They birthed that kinda woman
> that would make people's head spin
>
> I was born in Kansas
> and since I was young my fantas
> see was to be as fly as a toucan is
>
> When I was seven I put a ramp on my roof
> 'cause I swore I could soar
> But I just needed proof
> And I didn't own a sled
> So I used a box instead
> And glided from the roof and damn near cracked my head
> But it became the foundation
> of what I was chasin'
> the constant sensation
> of pure exhilaration
>
> Cut to 1920—the place was Long Beach Cali
> I took my first flight over the map of the valley
> and from that moment on it's like, "No more dilly dally
> I ain't some Silly Sally,

> I'm a pilot
> I'm a try it
> let's take a flight, shall we?"

(*Spoken*.) And then here comes the chorus.

(*Back to rapping*.)

> Yo it's time to Take Flight,
> it's time to Take Flight,
> I'm the enemy of gravity, up high's a great sight,
> it's time to Take Flight,
> it's time to Take Flight
> my body like serious situations
> I try to make light,
> It's time to Take Flight,
> I'm about to Take Flight,
> I'll stay chasing the sky like Ahab did the Great White.

Mr. Bugz   Woo! That was hot, yo. I'm feeling that.

Lamont   Yeah, it was decent.

Val   I like that *Moby-Dick* reference. We had to read that when I was a junior.

Nancy   I just—and here's my thing . . . (*To* **Val**.) And maybe you'll agree with me. I love rap so so so so so so so much. But it's kinda hard to justify some of it? You know? I mean even Snoop Dogg—who I adore—has said lines like, "Bitches ain't shit but hoes and tricks, lick on these nuts and suck the dick." And that's the chorus!

Val   And that's the chorus!

Nancy   Even Kanye, another genius, has said lines like, "And I know she like chocolate men, she got more . . . n-words . . . off than Cochran." So I just think it'd be really awesome to have a hip-hop show with like a positive strong female lead. To just like—counteract the majority of the misogyny that's embedded in hip-hop.

Val   I feel that.

Mr. Bugz   Do you, sista.

Lamont   Well, hold on. Hold on, hold on. (*Small pause*.) I mean, you know that . . . pss, whatever, never mind, I'm a get myself into trouble—

Nancy   Oh no no no, say whatever you want, please.

Lamont   Aight. You know that issues like . . . misogyny . . . hyper-masculinity . . . violence, all of that quote on quote "negative shit" . . . you know that makes up a *very small* but *very marketed* fraction of hip-hop content. You know that, right?

Nancy   Oh, right, yeah—

Lamont   The record labels, the corporations, they have an agenda that they are trying to push—

Nancy   Oh, I totally agree, totally. I am not trying to—I mean, yeah, I agree.

Lamont   Aight.

Nancy   But like. I mean—all of my favorite rappers—pretty much *every* amazing rapper you can think of has some sort of—

Gerry   Nancy, easy now—

Nancy   I'm just saying, like take you guys, who are my favorite group of all time, have the line, "That bitch can suck a dick like holy mackerel, I swear to God she could deep-throat a flagpole." Which I actually think is an incredible line, I'm just sayin'.

Mr. Bugz (*to* **Lamont**)   Now that line ain't Strictly. That line is *you*.

Lamont   Yup. That is me.

Val (*playfully*)   Yo, why you such a misogynist, Lamont?

Nancy   Oh no no no I'm not saying you're a misogynist, believe me—

Lamont   Yo, listen to me, aight. Label executives want you talkin' about guns and whores. Believe me. I've *been* in those meetings. My man Young Buck, you know Young Buck?

Nancy   I fucking love Young Buck!

Lamont   Young Buck had a song on his album that talks about police terrorism. You'd say that there's such a thing as police terrorism, correct?

Nancy   Oh, absolutely.

Lamont   Well, when the label heard that record they said "absolutely not." You cannot put that record on the album because it might create an environment that could put police officers' lives in danger.

Val   Yeah, I heard about that story.

Lamont   So they took the record off but *kept* the other fourteen songs on that album that talked about killing young black man. *That* they were fine with. And that is *not* what this hip-hop shit is about. When rappers talk about . . . selling crack, murder, all that dumb shit—I mean, I ain't gonna lie, I fuck with a lot of it 'cause a good song is a good song . . . but this hip-hop shit started as an *alternative* to gang violence, ya'namean?

Nancy   Yeah, definitely.

Lamont   But nowadays motherfuckas are disconnected from that, disconnected from the roots. Hip-hop for me is an extension of black aesthetic and the development into something higher, the same way Egypt came from Ethiopia, hip-hop is an extension of blues and the Negro spiritual. And that's how it is for me. I don't see hip-hop as the United Nations, okay? It ain't some multicultural melting pot. I see hip-hop as a *black genre*. But that's just me.

Pause.

Nancy   Wow. Just . . . you . . . I can't even argue with you, you are wise, man. You are just so wise.

Mr. Bugz   Come on now, man, there were some white people, Spanish people fucking with hip-hop back in the day—

Lamont   No there were not.

Mr. Bugz   I remember—

Lamont   Spanish people, maybe, yeah, there were a couple.

Val   First of all we are black, but we—

Lamont   / I know—

Val   —ain't gotta gripe over semantics right now—and there were more than a couple . . . fuckin' DJ Charlie Chase from Cold Crush, ain't that your favorite group?

Mr. Bugz   And there were more than a couple white boys too.

Lamont   Not to my recollection.

Mr. Bugz   Well, we remember shit differently.

Lamont   Yeah, I guess we do.

Val   Yo, ya'll sounding like some dinosaurs right now.

Nancy   You know . . . I also think it's interesting that—

Gerry   Anyway, what time is it? Shouldn't we—

Mr. Bugz   Nancy, you ever battle?

Nancy   I'm sorry?

Mr. Bugz   Battle rap. You ever, you know . . .

Nancy   Oh, uh, not in a long time. When I was in undergrad I won a freestyle competition though.

Mr. Bugz   Oh *word*? 'Cause you know . . . Val right here *battles*. At least she used to.

Val   I still do.

Mr. Bugz   Oh yeah? Well, uh . . .

Val   Why you trying to instigate?

Mr. Bugz   'Cause I'm a dick like that. You scared?

Val   Scared? *Me?*

Nancy   We don't have to do this, I mean it's been a while—

Lamont (*to* **Nancy**)   Are *you* scared?

Nancy   I mean . . . yeah, I am, but I think fear is a good thing.

Mr. Bugz   Well, there you go. This is hip-hop, right? Let's have us a little competition. Friendly, of course.

Pause. **Val** *and* **Nancy** *look at each other.*

Val   Aight.

Nancy   Sure.

Gerry   Do I really have to sit through this?

Mr. Bugz   Yeah, you do, you're gonna be a judge.

Lamont   Yup, he's right, there's three of us, so you gotta judge, Gerry with G.

Mr. Bugz   So pay attention.

Gerry   Jesus. (*Almost to himself as he goes and gets himself a beer.*) Making me watch people rap on a sidewalk, I can't *imagine* anything more appealing.

He gets a beer and pops it.

Fine, fuck it, go ahead, hurry up.

Val   You wanna go first?

Nancy   It's up to you.

Val   Whatever you want is cool with me.

Nancy   No, really, I honestly don't care.

Val   I mean it's an advantage to go second so why don't you—

Mr. Bugz   Yo, ya'll are being *way* too polite for two people about to battle, just hurry the fuck up and decide.

Val   But I mean, are we just doing one round?

Gerry   Only one round please for fuck's sake!

Val   Fine, I'll go first.

Nancy   Sounds good.

Mr. Bugz   Hold on, lemme put on a beat—make this official.

He goes to the boombox, plugs in his i-Pod and a beat comes on. Maybe "People's Champ" by OC and Apollo Brown

Val   You ready?

Nancy   I'm ready.

Val   Yo, yo, check it, yo, yo, check it, check it, check it, yo . . .

She takes a moment and then starts to rap.

> I said look at this white girl,
> you're a nice girl,
> but are you an emcee?
> or one of the Spice Girls,
> let me tell you something,
> your raps are straight nothing,
> fuck around with me you might get a concussion,
> now you seem pissed,
> I'm a make you scream bitch,
> this ain't your undergrad yo,
> this is Queens, bitch,
> so just accept the loss,
> or you're gonna get squashed,
> you're the human embodiment of an "oh my gosh,"
> You're the epitome of posh, get the fuck out my house,

or I'm a smack you with the silver spoon
that's stuck in your mouth,
yeah the name is Val
Kano, you're a child,
With a unibrow,
Get some tweezers and pluck that shit now.

Nancy   Wow. That was really good. Okay. I haven't done this in a long time so it may make no sense.

She bops her head and then starts to rap.

Yeah, your name is Val,
And right now,
homegirl you are not acting rationale,
I bet you got yourself a fat uncle named Sal,
who throws a beer can at his dog when he growls,
my rhymes gonna blast right through your ear canal
it's like a shootout at the OK Corral,
my friends all describe me as nice, but I'm fowl,
shall I keep insulting you? Yes I shall,
you dress like a dude, are you sure you're a gal?
you got a big bark but all I hear is a meow
I flow like wow,
an unheard of style

Mimes cocking a gun and shooting it.

Chick-chick-kapow,
I'm a rearrange your smile

Mr. Bugz   Wooooo! Goddamn!

Val *isn't done. She wants more.*

Val   Nah, nah, hold up, we going on again. Four bars back and forth, aight?

Nancy   Okay.

Val   Aight?

Nancy   Okay!

Val

> Lemme make this crystal clear,
> you ain't got no business here,
> Amelia Earhart, take flight and disappear,
> get the fuck outta here—'fo I make ya lights flicker,
> Lil' child looking ass, you too young to drink liquor

Nancy

> Too young to drink liquor?
> That's why I think quicker
> and girl you 'bout as tough as a pair of pink slippers,
> I'm rollin' up the swisher
> and smokin you ass,
> and I ain't never met nobody as broke as yo ass

Val

> Broke as my ass, have you seen this bitch please,
> with yo' mousey-looking face but still don't get no cheese,
> I'm a kill you with
> ease, this is straight murder,
> you weigh like fifty pounds go get yourself a burger

Nancy

> Get myself a burger—I guess we got beef,
> And I'm a be at your door sorta like a Christmas reef,
> so lemme say this again just woo the crowd,
> chick chick kapow, I'm a rearrange your smile

Mr. Bugz *bugs out (that's probably how he got his nickname). He stomps his feet on the floor, claps his hands, maybe even starts lightly punching* **Lamont** *in the arm he is so excited.*

Mr. Bugz   That shit was bananas!

Gerry (*actually impressed*)   Was all that all improvisational?

Mr. Bugz   You know it! Homegirl said, "chick chick kapow, I'm a rearrange your smile."

Nancy   That was really fun.

Val   Yeah.

Mr. Bugz   Fuck, that got me hype.

Val   Aight, so who won?

Pause.

Mr. Bugz (*to* **Lamont**)   You wanna go first?

Pause.

Lamont   You both were nice. But like—how do I put this? There's a lotta intricate details you gotta consider when judging a battle. For example . . . Nancy . . .

Nancy   Uh-huh . . .

Lamont   You got a decent flow, I ain't gonna front.

Nancy   Thank you.

Lamont   And you can think quick on your feet, aight, I'll give you that.

Nancy   Oh my God thank you so much.

Lamont   But when you said that gun line, to me it didn't seem authentic.

Nancy   It totally wasn't, I've never held a gun in my life.

Lamont   Well, you lose points then.

Nancy   That makes sense.

Lamont   I respond to things that are real. Ya'nahmean? Like when Val said pluck your unibrow, you know, not to embarrass you but you do got a little . . .

He taps in between his eyebrows.

Nancy   Yeah, I'm a quarter Italian.

Lamont   So, like I said, you were both nice. But my vote goes to Val.

Nancy   She was really good.

Mr. Bugz   Yo, who *gives* a fuck if she's ever held a gun or not, this is a *battle*.

Lamont   But I'm sayin'—

Mr. Bugz   Half the rappers these days are full of shit anyway, they don't actually live what they talking about.

Lamont   Yeah, well these days fuckin' suck, what else is new?

Mr. Bugz   Yo. Val. You know I think you're amazing . . .

Val   Uh-huh . . .

Mr. Bugz   But this girl edged ya. It was *close*. It was crazy close. But I give it to Nancy by like a nut hair. Just keeping it real.

Val (*grossed out*)   A nut hair?

Lamont   Well, Gerry with a G? You the tie breaker . . .

Pause.

Gerry   I have no *fucking* idea.

Mr. Bugz   Were you paying attention?

Gerry   I was trying to yes but—I'm not equipped to judge these things.

Lamont   Well, we need a tie breaker.

Gerry   Why? Is there a cash award, who gives a shit?

Nancy   I feel the same way. I don't care really who—

Lamont   Nah, fuck that, when there's a battle, there's gotta be a winner, that's just the way it is. So, who won?

Mr. Bugz   Nancy won.

Lamont   Well, I say Val won.

Mr. Bugz   Were you even paying attention to the battle, bro?

Lamont   How you gonna ask me if I was—Motherfucker, I *been* in battles, you never a spit a rhyme in your life.

Mr. Bugz   I've *hosted* battles, okay? I've seen emcees all across / the country-

Lamont   Like that really means / anything—

Mr. Bugz   I've seen *Biggie* battle live, did you ever see Biggie / Smalls battle—

Lamont   How can you not see that Val roasted her, even her demeanor, you know, the way she carried herself was / more official—

Mr. Bugz   Nancy said some creative ass shit, how you trying to front / on that?

Gerry   Alright, alright, alright, alright, alright, I'll decide, Jesus Christ.

Lamont *goes to grab another beer from the bag.*

Lamont (*half to himself*)   Telling me I wasn't paying attention . . .

Mr. Bugz   So, who you pick, Gerry?

Gerry   Well, let's see here . . .

As **Lamont** *walks back to where he was sitting, popping his beer can, he steps on* **Mr. Bugz***'s shoes.*

Mr. Bugz   Yo, what the *fuck*, man, you just stepped on my kicks!

Lamont   Oh shit, my fault.

Mr. Bugz   Goddamn, yo . . .

Bugz *spits on his hand and frantically starts rubbing his shoe.*

Mr. Bugz   . . . . look at this fuckin' mark you just made!

Lamont   I'm sorry, b, but you sitting with your legs all stretched out like—

Mr. Bugz   I'm sittin' how I always sit, how the fuck you gonna step on my kicks?

Lamont   I said I'm sorry.

Mr. Bugz   I just got these too.

Lamont   Well, you got another four hundred pair up in the crib so—

Mr. Bugz   But not *these*. These are expensive, man.

Val   Bugz, I never told you but I got those in the red.

Mr. Bugz (*with the same anger*)   I do too, but I like the blues more!

Lamont   Yo, I'm sorry I stepped on your shoes, b, it was an accident. Now, can we just finish this fuckin' judgin' shit already. Gerry, who you choose?

Long pause.

Gerry   You both . . . did a swell job. But if I had to say I'm . . . I'm gonna go with Val.

Lamont   Thank you.

Another pause.

Lamont (*to* **Nancy**)   Look, I'm not trying to say you were wack, 'cause you weren't—

Nancy   Oh, no it's totally cool—

Lamont   But this is hip-hop and you know in hip-hop, you gotta keep it real and not worry about hurting people's feelings.

Nancy   My feelings are not hurt, not at all.

Another pause.

Nancy (*to* **Val**)   Congratulations.

Val   Whatever, this was just a stupid battle.

Pause.

Lamont   I gotta take a leak. (*To* **Bugz**.) Can I get your keys?

A long pause. **Bugz** *looks at* **Lamont** *like he wants to crack him in the face. Because he does. He wants to crack him right in the nose. But instead he just slowly takes out his keys and hands them over.*

Lamont (*to* **Nancy**)   Nice meeting you.

Nancy   You too. Thank you, again, so much for meeting me.

Lamont   My pleasure.

Nancy   Okay this may be so corny but . . . would you mind taking a selfie with me?

Lamont *sighs.*

Lamont   Aight.

Nancy   Yay.

They take a selfie together.

Lamont   Just don't post that shit nowhere.

Nancy   Oh, no don't worry. And no pressure or anything, but if you wanna come see my show we run till the 28th.

Lamont   I'll tell you what . . . if Gerry recommends it . . . I'll come see it.

Nancy   Gotcha.

Lamont *exits into the building.*

Pause.

Gerry   Well . . . that was him. Should we get going, the trains are always a little fishy around this time?

Nancy   Yeah, I guess. . . . (*To* **Bugz**.) Hey, uh.

Mr. Bugz   Yo, lemme tell you something, Nancy. You doing your own thing. And I respect that.

Nancy   Thank you.

Mr. Bugz   Nah, I mean it. Just . . . keep doing what you do. Fuck the haters, you know what I'm sayin'? Just . . . keep being yourself.

Nancy   Thank you.

Val   Yeah, thank you, Bugz.

Mr. Bugz   Yo, how many times have I told you that you're nice? Huh? This is hip-hop, stop being so fucking sensitive.

Out of nowhere, **Bugz** *storms off down the block.*

Pause.

Nancy   I hope I didn't cause any—

Val   Don't worry about it.

Nancy   Okay. Well, uh. It was great to meet you.

Val   Yeah you too. We should battle again sometime.

Nancy   Oh, totally, yeah. Or we could just have a friendly cipher, we / don't-

Val   Nah, I wanna battle again.

Nancy   Totally. Yeah. That'd be cool. Look me up on the gram: Emcee Esher AKA Swagatha Christie.

Val *quickly looks her up.*

Val   Oh, damn, Rah Digga follows you?

Nancy   Oh my God, yeah, Rah Digga *judged the* freestyle competition I won in undergrad!

Val   We were on a track together couple years ago.

Nancy   Get out!

Val   Real talk, she's gotta be the most slept-on emcee of all time.

Nancy   So slept-on!

Val   Who your top five females?

Nancy   I mean, I feel like I gotta give the number one spot to Lauryn—

Val   Likewise.

Nancy   But MC Lyte and Latifah are the OGs so—

Gerry   NO MORE LISTS! For fuck's sake, please!

He taps his watch to **Nancy***, like "we gotta go."*

Val *hands her a card.*

Val   Check out my Soundcloud, all my info right there.

Nancy   Awesome!

They give each other a pound. **Nancy** *and* **Gerry** *exit.* **Val** *is alone. After a few beats* **Lamont** *comes back down.*

Lamont   Where the fuck is Bugz?

Val   He just walked off.

Lamont   But I got his keys.

Val *shrugs.* **Lamont** *opens another beer.*

Val   I think Bugz hates me.

Lamont   I think Bugz hates himself.

Val   He must find me . . . disgusting or something.

Lamont   Nah, girl, don't even say that.

Pause.

Val   You really thought I beat that girl?

Lamont *looks at* **Val** *like, "Are you crazy?"*

Lamont   Yeah. (*Pause.*) Do *you* think you beat that girl?

Beat.

Val (*meekly*)   Yeah. That girl was kinda good in her own way. I mean, we both were.

Another pause.

Lamont   You know . . . an executive from Epic Records was supposed to come to my nephew's show this Monday. But uh . . . he cancelled.

Val   He did?

Lamont   He listened to the album . . . he said he doesn't know how to market it. You believe that shit? My nephew talking about black pride, he talking about consciousness, he lyrical, he got word play. He talking about the shit KRS One was talking about, Rakim, Public Enemy. But this motherfucka from Epic Records . . . don't know how to market him. That's some shit, right?

But I'll tell you this. I'd bet you a million fuckin' dollars that if *Nancy* were to walk up into an office at Epic Records and spit one of her cute little raps, an executive would offer her a contract right then and there. Lemme tell you, Val, you are *five times* the emcee that girl is but they ain't no way in hell anyone gonna offer your Puerto Rican ass a record contract. Hell no.

But this just the world we live in. A world where Eminem is a genius. Eminem is nice, okay? He got talent. I can name fifty—yes fifty!—other rappers that are just as good if not better. But as soon as Eminem dropped his first album he on the cover of *Rolling Stone* magazine. I ain't never seen Talib Kweli on the cover of *Rolling Stone* magazine. Have you?

Val   Yo, you think Bugz is gay?

Lamont   What?

Val   I got some grub yesterday with this dude Charlie O who still works at the station. And the rumor that's going around the hallway is that Bugz got caught with a

prostitute . . . that was a *tranny*. And apparently this is like
the fourth time he's been arrested but the station keeps
covering it up, but now, on some publicity shit, Grand
Master Mason wants to interview him *on the air*, and like . . .
grill him about it. What the fuck, right?

Long pause.

Lamont   I think you should worry a little less about Bugz's
life. And focus on yourself.

Val   Yeah, well it's a little hard to focus on myself when you
just told me no one's gonna care about my Puerto Rican ass.

Lamont   Yeah, but *you* gotta care.

Val   I do! You don't think I do? You don't see every dime
I get going to the studio? You don't see me posting on the
gram, on TikTok, every two seconds, promoting, pushing
my shit on to everybody and they grandmother—two weeks
ago I took a fuckin' Greyhound to Bridgeport, Connecticut
just to go to an open mic, like I am *hungry*, b, my grind don't
stop, my grind do not stop.

Lamont   That's whassup then.

Val   These record companies can lick my Puerto Rican ass,
I'm a do this shit independent; get money without them.

Lamont   Yo, in this game, you gonna meet a lotta people
that are richer than you, that are more successful, and you
know what you say to them?

Val   Fuck you I rhyme better.

Lamont   Fuck you I rhyme better.

They pound.

Val   Lemme get up outta here. I'm a go take a bath. I gotta
exfoliate.

They give each other a pound. **Val** *exits on her Segway.*

Transition: **Lamont** *raps to the audience.*

Lamont
> Arm Leg Leg Arm Head, this God Body
> My Truth of Square where I stand
> My Squad By Me
> Hi, Nice to meet you
> There's some things I'd like to teach you
> Step One—go over there and join the other sheeple
>
> Step Two—take this gun and shoot
> your brother over there's got tons of loot
>
> Number three—our record company
> loves hearing about all the bitches that you see
>
> Numero quatro—you could never have enough macho
> Plus the blood in yo' veins is as cold as gazpacho
>
> The fifth and most important on the list
> We don't like that image of you raising your fist
> That's stuff from the past and a bit too racial
> And something a lotta consumers won't relate to
> Follow these rules you'll have mad bread to break up
> Don't? You might have to see a little pay cut
> It's your choice, homie, so what you say? Say what?
> . . . Shit, ya'll need to wake up . . .

We segue to a couple hours later.

Lamont *still sits.* **Bugz** *approaches from down the block.*

Lamont   Yo.

Mr. Bugz   Yo.

Lamont   Where you been at?

Mr. Bugz   Strolling. You just been sitting here?

Lamont   Yup. (*Small pause.*) We need to talk, yo.

Mr. Bugz   Yeah, I guess we do.

Lamont   I've heard these rumors that . . . Mason wants to interview you on the air about some shit. That true?

Pause. **Bugz** *nods*.

Lamont   So, what you thinking?

Pause.

Mr. Bugz   I mean, I *have* to do the interview. Or else they're gonna fire me for good.

Lamont   Nah, I mean what you thinking about *saying*.

Pause. **Bugz** *take a big, big breath*.

Mr. Bugz   Honestly . . . I'm thinking about . . . telling the truth.

Lamont   And what is the truth?

Mr. Bugz   The truth? The truth, the truth, the truth . . . sometimes it's hard to know what the truth is.

Lamont   What are the facts?

Mr. Bugz   The facts . . . are that I have been arrested. . . . on several occasions . . . for soliciting . . . transexual prostitutes. (*Pause.*) I've only gotten head from them. I've always I've been pitching, never catching. I have never had intercourse with a man I have never—

Lamont   How long this been going on?

Mr. Bugz   I don't know. Since maybe around the time Velotta and I separated. I was just so tired of dealing with that shit, you know? So I started going to strip clubs on the regular. Like every night, you know, I was like, addicted to strip clubs. Then one day I was like . . . lemme try this . . .

Lamont   "Lemme try this"?

Mr. Bugz   It's hard to explain.

Pause.

Lamont   Were you molested as a kid or some shit?

Mr. Bugz   Nah.

Lamont   I'm just trying to—you don't have any like, traumatic—

Mr. Bugz   I've loved pussy my whole life, dawg. You *know* that. You've *seen* me with women.

Pause.

Lamont   So, what, you're a . . . a bisexual?

Mr. Bugz   I don't know what I am.

Lamont   You don't *know*?

Mr. Bugz   It's like . . . put it like this. Sometimes you hear a certain record . . . you're like, is this a hip-hop record or an R&B record? I'm not sure.

Pause.

Lamont   Aight. I get it.

Mr. Bugz   You get it?

Lamont   Well, look, man. You wanna know the truth? You wanna know the absolute truth? I've always had an inkling- just a little little *inkling*—in the back of my mind, about your . . . (*Struggling to find the right way to phrase it.*) . . . proclivities, let's say. And once I became aware of it—you wanna know the truth? Once I was aware of it . . . I almost respected you even more. You know why? (*Pause.*) 'Cause you kept that shit to yourself. If you were a, a, Broadway singer or whatever, or maybe even a house music kinda dude then, yeah, by all means, flaunt that shit. But you not. You a legendary hip-hop DJ. So, you kept that shit on the low. Why? 'CAUSE THAT'S. NOT. HIP-HOP. IT'S JUST NOT. YOU *KNOW* IT'S NOT. You gotta think, man, you admit to the world that you a homosexual, what kinda message that's gonna send? Little gay kids everywhere, "Ooh, I'm a homosexual too. Lemme pick up a microphone. Lemme talk about fucking dudess in the ass in my rhymes," next thing you know, this whole motherfuckin' industry is *flooded* with them . . . and then where's the essence? Huh? Where's the *foundation* . . . of this hip-hop shit? It's *already* happening. I mean, who the fuck started this shit, man? *Us*. *Black* males. *Alpha* black males. And who was I just getting lectured to about how hip-hop should *be*? Some *goddamn* little white girl. It's all connected, man.

Mr. Bugz   She wasn't *lecturing* you—

Lamont   Like she knows anything about the struggle that hip-hop came from, like she—

Mr. Bugz   She just wanted to hang out with you, man, she didn't—

Lamont   And that Amelia Earhart shit sounds like a stupid fucking idea.

Mr. Bugz   I thought it was tight. I can't lie. I thought it was clever.

Lamont   Amelia Earhart and hip-hop? Gimme a goddamn break. It's like that Langston Hughes poem, man, they're bringing my blues to Broadway. You know that poem?

He quotes from "Notes on Commercial Theatre."

Look that shit up. Written in 1940 something. Same shit going on now.

Long pause.

Mr. Bugz   I'm not a homosexual.

Lamont   Goddamn right you're not.

Mr. Bugz   But I have had . . . I have gotten . . . oral sex from—

Lamont   No you haven't.

Mr. Bugz   Yes, I have.

Lamont   Well, no one needs to know that. What you do in your personal life is your own goddamn business and don't need to be broadcast on the radio for every motherfuckah to hear.

Mr. Bugz   I can't keep this secret anymore, man. I feel like I been in a cage, man, and . . . I don't know . . . I just don't know . . . I feel . . . I feel . . .

Lamont   You don't understand the repercussions, b. You really don't. You don't understand the kinda weight your name carries, you don't understand what a titan you are in this hip-hop shit. As one of the . . . architects of this hip-hop shit. Now, you gonna think about yourself? And ya *feelings*? Or you gonna think about this culture that you built? That needs to be preserved.

Small pause.

Mr. Bugz   I gotta live my truth, dawg. I just gotta live my truth.

Lamont   Well, I gotta live mine and tell you that if you talk about this shit on the air you are making a big fucking mistake. You can do whatever you want in your private life, b. Whatever you want, and fuck it, I don't judge you. You my man. But it ain't nobody's business. Just keep that shit to yourself.

Mr. Bugz   I BEEN KEEPING THIS SHIT TO MYSELF AND LOOK WHERE THE FUCK IT GOT ME. COMMITTING A FUCKING CRIME. GETTING FUCKING ARRESTED. I BEEN KEEPING IT TO MYSELF, DAWG, THE FUCK YOU THINK I BEEN DOING?

Lamont   Yo, Bugz, I love you, b. You're my brother and I love you. Your whole life, everything you've represented, everything you stand for everything I stand for . . . that's gonna all get forgotten in ten years.

Mr. Bugz   What if my whole life has been a lie though?

Lamont   Ten years from now the movie of the year will be the hip-hop fuckin' version of *La La Land* . . . you know who's gonna be the center of that movie? Not us. Not us.

Mr. Bugz   Not you.

Lamont   Oh, so you on their side?

Mr. Bugz   What fuckin' sides, b, what fuckin' sides are you talking about, man? We on the same side!

Lamont   I love you, Bugz—

Mr. Bugz   You keep saying that—

Lamont   But if . . .

Mr. Bugz   No buts! We done with that, it's I love you *period*.

Lamont   If you talk about this shit on the air? I just. . . . (*Long pause*.) . . . I just don't know if I could fuck with you anymore. I'll always love you. But yo . . .

He just shakes his head.

Mr. Bugz   Can I get my keys?

Pause. **Lamont** *gives him the keys*. **Bugz** *is about to head into the building*.

Mr. Bugz   Yo, man, would you give a fuck about this if you were still relevant? Rappers that are actually *making a living*, you really think they care about my sexuality? Huh? If you weren't living in your younger sister's basement on 50th Avenue right now I have a feeling your outlook might be a lot different. 'Cause I can think of plenty of black alpha males that are killing the game right now *but you ain't one of them*. So *fuck* your backwards way of thinking, bro.

Pause.

Lamont   Man . . . just do what you gotta do. Go on the air. Say what you gotta say. (*Pause*.) And be grateful your mom won't be able to understand it.

Bugz *exits into the building*.

Lamont *takes a deep breath. He goes over to the scaffolding, does some pull-ups. He can only do five*.

The blinds of **Bugz***'s window are lifted up for the first time in the play. We see* **Bugz** *staring out the window at* **Lamont***.*

When **Lamont** *is done with the pull-ups he slowly meanders back to the stoop.*

As **Lamont** *crosses under the window,* **Bugz** *opens it . . .*

Mr. Bugz   Yo, my man . . .

As **Lamont** *looks up* **Bugz** *ducks down and reappears with a giant bucket.*

He leans out the window and dumps the entire bucket of red liquid down on **Lamont***, completely drenching him.*

Lamont   YO, WHAT THE FUCK, B!

Mr. Bugz   THAT'S FOR STEPPIN' ON MY FUCKIN' SNEAKERS!

Bugz *ducks back into his apartment, shuts the window.*

Lamont (*shouting, furiously*)   Come down here, yo! You fuckin' bitch! Yo, Bugz! BUGZ! You fuckin' pussy! Oh my God.

He goes to the buzzer and buzzes over and over again. Goes back and shouts up the window.

I swear to God, I ain't leaving till you come down here.

Nothing. He starts to feel the substance on his body.

What the fuck is this, man, Kool-Aid? How the fuck you got a bucketful of Kool-Aid up in your crib, you unhealthy motherfucker! FUCK!

He sits back down. Long, long pause. **Gerry** *enters from down the block.*

Gerry   What the hell happened to you?

Lamont   Yo, you got a cigarette, man?

Gerry   I most certainly do.

He takes out a pack and gives **Lamont** *a cigarette. He lights up.*

Gerry   Are you . . . are you hurt?

Lamont   I'm fine, yo.

Gerry   Did you need to come take a shower?

Lamont   I'm *fine,* yo. (*Takes a beat.*) Thank you.

Another pause.

Gerry   Well, then. Goodnight.

Lamont   Goodnight.

Gerry *goes into his building. A long, long pause. Eventually* **Gerry** *comes back down with a towel. Hands it to* **Lamont**.

Gerry   I'm sorry but you just look ridiculous, please take this.

Lamont *takes it and starts to dry himself off.* **Gerry** *sits down next to him. Lights up another cigarette. Takes a pause. Stretches his neck. Rubs it.*

Gerry   Ahh . . .

Lamont   You aight?

Gerry   Yeah just . . . hurt my neck last night.

Lamont   What happened?

Gerry   Just uh. Slept funny. My pillows suck.

Lamont   Gotta get yourself a shredded memory foam pillow by Xtreme Comforts. Telling you. It'll change your life.

Gerry   Thanks. I'll look into it.

Pause.

He takes out the spinner and spins it on his finger. **Lamont** *sees this. Watches but says nothing.*

Gerry   So were you and your uh . . . you know . . . your wacky friends doing some ritual?

Lamont   What?

Gerry   You know, your wacky friends that are around here sometimes.

Lamont   The gods?

Gerry   Right. The gods.

Lamont   Nah, man. Nah.

Gerry   What are you guys anyway? A cult?

Lamont   Nah, man, we ain't a cult.

Gerry   A group?

Lamont   Kind of a group, yeah.

Gerry   And what do you believe in?

Lamont   We believe 85 percent of the population are deaf, dumb, and blind. That they lack knowledge of self. 10 percent of the population have this knowledge but hide it from the rest. That leaves the 5 percent. The poor righteous teachers. Who try and liberate the minds of the 85 percent.

Small pause.

Gerry   Huh.

He takes a long drag of his cigarettes.

Those numbers sound about right. And you're pro-black?

Lamont   We are pro-black. We believe that the Original Man is a black man. The Asiatic Black man.

Gerry   And why the heck are you always calling yourself gods? Seems a bit arrogant to me.

Lamont   We don't believe in some mystery god up in the sky. We believe that every black man is his *own* god. His own

ALLAH. Arm Leg Leg Arm Head. That's an acronym for Allah. (*Gesturing to himself.*) God body.

Gerry   Huh. But you're not anti-white? You don't hate white people, you don't think that the white man is the devil?

Pause.

Lamont   Are you asking me . . . if I hate *you*, Gerry? Is that what you're *actually* asking . . .

Small pause.

Gerry   I couldn't care *less* . . . who *hates* me. Let me to tell you something, there are thousands . . . *thousands and thousands* . . . of people who hate me out there and I wouldn't for one second give them the honor of entering one of my thoughts.

Lamont   I had a song called "America's Most Hated." Did you know that?

Gerry   Good for you.

Pause.

Lamont   Look, do I hate every single white person on this earth, no of course not. But do I think that the white man is the devil? Absolutely.

Gerry   I thought so.

Lamont   But now see . . . when we speak of god and devil, we not talking about it how you may think. Ain't no religious undertones to it, we talking about the white man of *mind*, the *white mind*, the one that murders and rapes and steals, the unrighteous mind . . . that's the devil. And that can be within all different skin colors of people.

Gerry   Huh.

He takes a big drag of his cigarette.

Gerry   I need to get the fuck outta this city.

Lamont   Shit, you and me both.

Gerry   Fucking hate New York. If I had my druthers I'd be living on some, I don't know, some villa somewhere. In Italy. But I'm broke.

Lamont   I heard you used to be a millionaire.

Gerry   Yup.

Lamont   So what the fuck happened?

Gerry   Life. Or rather . . . the fear of losing it.

Lamont   Huh?

Gerry   Look . . . you're basically a kid. You don't know what it was like to be someone of my age, going through what we did.

Lamont   How old *are* you?

Gerry   No one knows. Old enough to not have any more friends.

Lamont   Shit, half my boys were gone before twenty-five.

Gerry   I'm not sure if you remember this thing called the 1980s. But in the 1980s. The people in my circle. Were all. Dying. And I was convinced that I was next. The amount of shit that I did, the people I was with . . . I didn't even have to find out . . . I *knew*, okay? I *knew*. Do you have any idea what that's like? To know you could die, I mean actually die any day?

Lamont   I'm a black man in America. You really asking me that question?

Gerry   So I said fuck it! I'm traveling the world.

Lamont   Shit, I racked up some serious stamps on my passport too.

Gerry   Brussels, Berlin, Prague, drinks for him, drinks for her, drinks for the bartender, drinks for the homeless guy outside, plus a steak dinner, who gives a shit! I was—as you and your friends like to say—I was balling!

Lamont   That's what's up.

Gerry   Shit, I was spending money like there wasn't even a yesterday.

Lamont (*holds up his watch*)   See this? Five grand. Advance from the record company. Before they fucked me and my group in the ass. Bought it in '92.

Gerry   Why not!

Lamont   Why the fuck not? Motherfuckers telling me to invest, I'm like, "I don't know where I'm gonna be in five years. I don't know where I'm gonna be next week."

Gerry   People. Fucking. Suck.

Lamont   Word.

Long pause.

So what was you up to tonight?

Gerry   I just saw Nancy's show.

Lamont   And?

Gerry   Well, first of all. *Val* showed up. She sat right next to me. Before the show started I had to make more small talk, my least favorite thing of all time.

Lamont   But you *know* Val.

Gerry   I know Val *here*. On this *stoop*. It was very bizarre seeing her in a different setting. Like running into your psychiatrist on the beach.

Lamont   Aight. Well, how was the show?

Another pause.

Gerry I gotta be honest with ya, Lamont. And I hate to admit this. I truly, truly hate to admit this. But I was proud of her. I'm thinking, here is this girl who works so hard . . . who works so fucking hard, who is trying something new, who is trying to reinvent something, something that takes guts and insight and and . . . (*Small pause.*) You know, in an odd way it got me thinking about my old friend Bob. Bob was in the military, you know? And believe it or not, he was one of those mean and tough kind of drill sergeants. Like from that movie uh, uh . . . (*Snapping his fingers.*) . . . what's that movie that I hate? The one by Stanley Kubrick?

Lamont *Full Metal Jacket*?

Gerry Like *Full Metal Jacke*t. The drill sergeant in that . . . that was Bob Ross. He screamed so much in the military that once he got out he vowed to never scream again. And so what did he do? The opposite of screaming. Painting. Painting mountains and skies and happy little trees. He completely reinvented himself. It wasn't easy either. No one wanted to pick up his show at first. "We're just gonna sit there and watch you paint? Who the hell is gonna wanna watch that?" So to save money he got his hair permed. Did you know that? So he wouldn't have to spend on hair cuts. That's how he got his world-famous hair. Most people don't know that. (*Small beat, smiling.*) He did his own thing, Bob. He really did. (*Another beat.*) I was in love with that man. Full blown, eyes as big as the fuckin' moon in love.

Lamont *listens.*

Gerry So, tonight, I'm sitting there . . . and . . . (*Takes a deep breath.*) I'm watching her on stage rippity rappin' her tits off and I thought to myself, "God . . . I am really, really proud." Hats off, Nancy. And everyone liked it. Standing ovation. They really, *really* liked it.

Another pause.

Lamont Yeah, but . . . did *you* like it?

Gerry *takes a little breath.*

Then blows a large raspberry.

Lamont *smirks. He extends his fist out to* **Gerry**. **Gerry** *extends his fist out to* **Lamont**.

They bump fists.

End of play.